Witnesses to an Execution

CAIAPHAS

The Pernicious High Priest

Volume 3

Michael W. Dewar

Copyright © 2025 by Michael W. Dewar, Sr.
All rights reserved. No part of this book may be reproduced in any form without written permission from the author or publisher.

Published in the United States by:
Dwelling Place Publishers
PO Box 360196
Brooklyn, NY 11236

DPSCleansing.com

ISBN: 979-89928854-2-2 (Paperback)
ISBN: 979-89928854-3-9 (eBook)

Unless otherwise indicated, Bible quotations are taken from The Holy Bible, New International Version (NIV). Copyright © 1973, 1978, 1984 by International Bible Society; The Holy Bible, King James Version(KJV or NKJV); The Holy Bible, ESV, and The Holy Bible, New Living Translation(NLT). Copyright © 1996 by Tyndale House Publishers, Inc.

Dedicated

Dedicated to the honor of those who are called and commissioned to shepherd God's people as pastors and deacons or elders. May they be faithful as servants in the execution their charge to the glory of God and in honor our Lord Jesus Christ, the Chief Shepherd.

People should always pray and not lose heart. "But when the Son of Man comes, will He find faith on the earth?"
(Luke 18:8).

CONTENTS

PREFACE..vii

INTRODUCTION...9

CHAPTER 1..13
WHO WAS CAIAPHAS?

CHAPTER 2..23
PRIESTHOOD, ELDERS, AND THE TEMPLE

CHAPTER 3..37
THE TEMPLE ADMINISTRATION

CHAPTER 4..45
CAIAPHAS THE HUNTER

CHAPTER 5..61
THE FUTURE OF THE TEMPLE PREDICTED

CHAPTER 6..71
CHIAPHAS IN THE DEATH AND RESURRECTION COVERUP OF THE CHEIST

CHAPTER 7..83
JUDAISM WITHOUT TEMPLE AND SACRIFICE

REFERENCES..99

OTHER BOOKS BY THIS AUTHOR.....................103

ABOUT THE AUTHOR......................................107

PREFACE

This is the third volume in the series, *Witnesses to an Execution*. It explores and exposes the religious leadership of Israel in *First Century* AD and their witting culpability in the execution of Jesus of Nazareth, the Messiah. At the very pinnacle of that leadership structure was God's high priest, Caiaphas.

Caiaphas was the one who presided over the religious trial of Jesus, charged Him with blasphemy, and declared Him worthy of death. Yet, he did not order Jesus executed the Jewish way, by stoning as he would other blasphemers, like Stephen. Because it was not a politically expedient thing to do. Jesus was popular among the common people, and it would spark a riot.

Pilate, the Roman governor, exercised the prerogative of pardon as well as conducting civil trials and executing criminals. Jesus was called, King of the Jews, a title that He did not publicly claim or deny. But it was the civil charge Caiaphas and his group brought to Pilate and demanded the death penalty, crucifixion.

Over the centuries, the role of the Jewish high priest, the chief priests, the elders, and the Sanhedrin have been smoothly glossed over to mask the Jewish culpability in the death of the

Nazarene. One reason is the fear of a vigorous antisemitism backlash. Antisemitism is a corrosive evil that must be fiercely fought. But one should not use the fear of one evil to cover up another evil. That is, the evil of an innocent man put to death on false charges because He made some people uncomfortable.

Some popular evangelical pastors and tele-evangelists have placed the crucifixion of the Christ squarely in the hands of the Roman governor, but they overlooked that the governor was pushed by powerful men who already had an agenda to kill Jesus. But they wanted Him dead the Roman way, not the Jewish way. Only the governor could legally do it the Roman way.

But having tried Jesus, the governor found Him innocent and declared such innocence no less than three times. The governor wanted to set Jesus free, but Caiaphas and his group rallied the crowd to shout, "Crucify Him!"

They finally threw the governor a political hand grenade, "We have no king but Ceasar!" If you set this man free, you are not Caesar's friend. They forced the governor's hand by threatening his position. Pilate capitulated and gave them what they wanted, the crucifixion of the Nazarene.

On the one hand, this book examines the facts, refutes the lies, and exposes the truth to the light of day. On the other hand, this book warns that what Jewish leaders did in first century AD should not be used to promote hate or antisemitism in the twenty-first century and beyond. That is not what our Lord wants. He taught love as the new commandment and His trademark for true discipleship is "Love thy neighbor as thyself!"

INTRODUCTION

This is the third volume in the series, *Witnesses to an Execution*. Caiaphas was more than an eye-witness to the murder of the Christ. From a human perspective, he was the chief participant in plotting the murder.

Therefore, he is not a willing witness. He is what the legal system today calls, a hostile witness. If it were possible to swear him-in, his testimony would not be credible. Perhaps, he would plead the fifth because of fear of self-incrimination. He was the one that paid the hit-man Judas and again paid off the soldiers to cover up the truth of the resurrection.

Judas has come down to us from antiquity as one of the lowest scums among humans that every lived. He was the man who excused himself from the Last Supper Table at such a sacred hour to cut the betrayal deal with the enemies of Jesus for thirty pieces of silver. The price of a slave.

But there was another scum behind the scenes, pulling the strings like a puppet master. His name is Caiaphas, the high priest. He might be worse than Judas because he had cause, motives, and resources. He had access to a police force and

CAIAPHAS *The Pernicious High Priest*

abundance of cash to finance any nefarious activity his heart desired. He was committed to the demise of the Nazarene. But Caiaphas is often glossed over, not given the full credit he deserves in successfully plotting the murder of the Christ, even though his treachery is clearly documented in all four gospels.

Have you ever wondered why some evangelical preachers, Bible scholars and theologians are often so quick to transition from the human wickedness side of Jesus' death to the divine side? The quick answer is this: the divine side provides more fertile soil to do theology. There is another reason; it is an attempt to shield Caiaphas' ancestry from their culpability in the murder of the Christ.

But this work is not going to give Caiaphas a quick out of jail card because of the divine hand in Jesus' death. The purpose of God to have Joseph in Egypt did not reduce the wickedness of what his brothers did to him and their father Jacob. Neither can heaven or earth gloss over Caiaphas' treachery against Jesus.

There are those today who would like to soften the Jewish ancestral wicked role in the murder of Jesus to soften modern antisemitism, but one wickedness cannot cover for another. Both must be exposed for what they are—wickedness!

Jesus was Jewish, so was His disciples, including Judas. Caiaphas the high priest was also Jewish. These are indisputable facts of history. The cancer to murder may have had two hosts: Caiaphas and Judas and for two different reasons. On Judas' part, he did not want Jesus dead. He wanted Jesus to use His extraordinary powers to liberate Israel from the oppressive Roman yoke or his greed and love for money moved him to make some extra money on the side or both.

Introduction

Judas had witnessed Jesus gotten out of threats on His life many times before. If it comes down to that, he calculated, Jesus will get away again. But when Judas discovered that Jesus was not going to escape this time, *he change his mind* and sought to cancel the transaction. *He repented himself* (Matt.27:3-4 KJV).

But Caiaphas and his group were not willing to change their position, so they rebuffed him instead. To them, Judas was dispensable; they used him to accomplish their wickedness and disposed of him like a useless piece of dirty rags.

Judas is now awakened to the gravity of his crime. And since they would not take back the money and drop the charges against Jesus, Judas threw down the money in the Temple and rushed to hang himself (Matt.27:5). From Judas' perspective, it was a transaction that went bad. Whatever his reason, liberation ideals or greed for money, the corrosive malignancy that took root in his heart also had another host which was Caiaphas.

Judas knew that and that is why he went to Caiaphas to profit from this scheme. From Caiaphas the cancer quickly spread and took root in the body of the Sanhedrin where it metastasized, sparing *only a few tissues*. Caiaphas and his group wanted to kill Jesus before Judas made it easy.[1] On the Sanhedrin, only Nicodemus and Joseph of Arimathea did not vote to have Jesus terminated (Matt.27:57-60; Luke 23:50-54; John 19:38-42).

Terminated is a nice word but it makes what happened seems benign. But in this context, it means murder. Not killed because that is reserved for nation State at war; not manslaughter, because Jesus was innocent and His death was premeditated, carefully plotted. It was murder from a human perspective.

Though elegantly dressed in religious vestment, Caiaphas had a murderous heart; he was a wolf in sheep's clothing. He convinced his colleagues on the Sanhedrin that it was a good thing killing one man to save the nation rather than the whole nation perish (John 11:49-50). He tried to find a plausible justification to get around, *You shall not murder* (Exodus 20:13).

Caiaphas called money Judas returned, *blood money*; that further confirms they were not oblivious to the wickedness of the enterprise they had undertaken to murder an innocent man.

This book is an attempt to force out Caiaphas from the shadows and from behind religious vestment to shoulder the full generational curse levied upon the entire Jewish people.

During the civil trial of Jesus, Pilate offered to release Jesus, but Caiaphas and the crowd chose the terrorist Barabbas instead. Pilate then asked, "What then shall I do with Jesus who is called the Messiah?" They shouted, "Crucify him!" "All the people answered, His blood is on us and on our children!" (Matt.27:21-25). Caiaphas was wicked, selfish, greedy, and myopic man. He chose to preserve his own position and wealth over the interests of his own people. He released a curse on his posterity.

Just as Judas serves as a warning to the divinity student, the vocational minister, and to all who follow Jesus, Caiaphas plays a similar role to religious leaders who all claim to represent God. But if we are not careful, we end up representing Satan instead. Caiaphas occupied the highest religious office among God's people in first century Israel but his fall from grace was more like that of Lucifer's. Religious titles do not give us immunity from the corrosive effects of sin.

CHAPTER 1

WHO WAS CAIAPHAS?

Caiaphas was the high priest and chairman of the Jewish High Council that presided over the religious trial of Jesus, leading to His public execution. It happened about AD 33 in first century Jerusalem. He loathed Jesus and wanted hm dead!

Caiaphas viewed Jesus as this troublemaker from the Galilee region, an unlettered, itinerant preacher/healer from the peasant village of Nazareth who was popular with the common people. Caiaphas insisted that Jesus could not be the Messiah because no prophet had ever come out of Galilee but of the lineage of king David (John 7:40-52). His implication is that Jesus was not from the right geography or had the right ancestral connection.

The high priest, therefore, considered it his duty to silence this ambitious, revolutionary upstart, get rid of Him permanently by all necessary means. But this must be done by stealth and subtilty, so as not to excite his supporters. They were among the common people. This was Caiaphas' broad rationale.

But on a more earthy level who was Caiaphas? What was his family background? In what social and religious soil was he nurtured, and what was his ambition? This chapter uncovers the answer to these questions and more.

Caiaphas, the Man

Much is not known about the birth, immediate family tree, and upbringing of Caiaphas, except that the *high priest* position he grew up to occupy would place him in the Aaronic branch of the tribe of Levi (Ex.28:1-30). Aaron, the brother of Moses, was the first high priest, and his four sons were priests under him while he was alive and priests after he was dead (Ex.29).

The Lord declared that the priesthood belong to the family of Aaron and to that lineage only. By divine order that would be a "lasting ordinance" in Israel (verse 9). So, the priesthood was by hereditary and exclusive to the Aaronic family as stipulated in the Torah. This is also confirmed in secular history. For example, the historian, Flavius Josephus writes:

> In the first place, therefore, history informs us that Aaron, the brother of Moses, officiated to God as a high priest; and that after his death, his sons succeeded him immediately; and that this dignity hath been continued down from them all to their posterity….it is a custom in our country that no one should take the high priesthood of God, but he who is of the blood of Aaron, while

everyone who is of another stock, though he were a king, can never obtain the high priesthood.[1]

Therefore, by virtue of his office of *high priest,* we may conclude that Caiaphas was from the tribe of Levi and from the lineage of Aaron. Caiaphas is said to be a "surname which was originally drawn from Joseph," but became "the ordinary and official designation and was used for the name."[2]

Caiaphas was married to the daughter of Annas who preceded him in the office of high priest but continued to wield significant power and influence during Caiaphas' tenure. The fact that the arresting guards first brought Jesus to Annas, the father-in-law of Caiaphas, shows that Annas, as high priest *emeritus,* continued to have significant power and influence on the Sanhedrin (John 18:12-14).

In honor, he is called high priest even when out of office, as a President of the United States retains the title even when out of office. Caiaphas had sons that followed him in the office of high priest. What we know of this man's character is what was revealed during his tenure as high priest.

Caiaphas, the High Priest

As part of the Jewish aristocracy, the high priest, the chief priests, and elders were the guardian of Israel's faith, traditions, and culture. They were the custodians of divine revelation, the books of the Torah (the Law) handed down from God through Moses. It was the constitution of the Hebrew nation.

The leaders of the people were told not to turn to the left or right-hand from obeying the teachings and precepts of the Law.

CAIAPHAS The Pernicious High Priest

By their practice of obedience, they would have good success and prosperity (Jos.1:8-11). The skeletal foundation of the moral Law is what we know as the Ten Commandments (Ex.20:1-20?). Israel's most frequent sin was idolatry. Moses in his departure speech strongly warned them that their very survival as a nation is contingent on their obedience to God's Law to which blessings and curses were enjoined. There were blessings for obedience and curses for disobedience (Deu.28).

The priesthood evolved over time. By the time of Jesus, the high priest was like the CEO and chairperson of the board, he stood head and shoulders above the chief priests and elders of the people as the chief gatekeepers of the divine order. These men were members of the powerful *Jewish High Council*, the Sanhedrin which had control over Jewish life.

The whole nation of Jews looked to the high priest as the representative and mediator between God and his people. This reality was represented by twelve precious stones representing the twelve tribes fixed into breast-piece of the high priest vestment and worn over his heart as he performed his priestly duties before God (Ex.29:15-30).

Caiaphas was the Jewish high priest during the reign of Tiberius Caesar when Jesus began His public ministry. He presided over the activities leading to the arrest, trials, and execution of Jesus Christ (Luke 3:2; Matt.26:1-5, 57).[3]

Caiaphas was appointed to the position of high priest by the Curator Valerius Gratus and remained in that office through the entire governorship of Pontius Pilate. But was terminated by the "Proconsul Vitellus about AD 38."[4] When Pilate arrived in Judea to begin his tenure as Procurator, Caiaphas was already high priest and retained the position to the end of Pilate's twelve-year tenure. He was high priest for eighteen years.[5]

Caiaphas was a rich man, influential, powerful, and crafty to remain in office of high priest that long. One must have money and influence to buy off the governor to get appointed and retain the office. The office itself would make the holder much richer. The position was a one-year political appointment, but the incumbent could be reappointed any number of times.

Caiaphas, the Politician

The position of high priest was highly political. The person chosen for this office must know the needs and traditions of his own people, the local politics, and to some extent the politics of Rome. At least, know Ceasar's expectation for this region.

The fact that Israel was under Roman occupation, the high priest was appointed yearly by the governor, a politician, and served at his pleasure. Therefore, the high priest must be able to skillfully balance the interests of Ceasar and the interest of his own people, Israel. The interest of the whole Hebrew nation was riding on this delicate balance of religion and politics. The stakes were high on both sides.

But the personal stakes were high for both the governor and the high priest. Both maintained their enormous wealth and power by the positions they held, and both could jeopardize the position of the other. The governor was ruthless and Ceasar was ruthless; their mood, interest, and preference could change anytime for good or evil. In most cases, for evil.

To retain tenure, the successful high priest must know how to please the governor, not overly threaten his position with whatever personal influence one may have with Caesar. The remarkable length of Caiaphas' tenure" is a testimony to "his tremendous wealth, political power, and shrewdness." [6]

Eugenia S. Constantinou observes that "Jewish high priests were not chosen by Roman governors because they had the requisite family lineage, nor because they were pious and devout. They attained this position through wealth, influence, political savvy, ruthlessness, and brutality."[7]

Because of this, the position of the priesthood and Judaism for that matter became grossly corrupted. That corruption and departure from its original purpose and orthodoxy, placed the priesthood and Judaism on a collision course with Jesus of Nazareth and His ministry.

Caiaphas and Jesus

We know of Caiaphas because of his connection with Jesus, that connection dominates Caiaphas life for time and eternity. We have already established that Caiaphas was corrupted and presided over a corrupted priesthood and religious system.

Jesus came on the scene and sought to correct and cleanup this corrupted system, but the elite gatekeepers of the faith and its institutions would have none of it. They steadfastly resisted His efforts. This conflict is evident through the synoptic gospels, which are Matthew, Mark, and Luke. The conflict is also evident in John's gospel. They questioned the legitimacy of His birth, the source of His miraculous power, the authority of His Messianic claims, and His claim to divinity (Matt.12:1-13, 22-45, 21:23-27; John 6: 41-59).

WHO WAS CAIAPHAS?

Jesus was repeatedly rebuffed by the religious elites. The high priest, the chief priests, the elders, and others of the elite class considered Him a thorn in their sides, and a fly in their ointment. They felt He was a threat to their comfortable position with Rome. For these, among other reasons, they laid political and religious traps for Him. But Jesus proved much too smart to fall into their traps. They could not take Him until His time had come. His incarnation was on a divine schedule (Luke 4: 28-29).

"Is it lawful to pay taxes to Caesar?" This was a trick question, to trap Jesus, politically. Jesus asked for a coin that they used to pay taxes. He held it up and asked, "Whose image and inscription is on this coin?" They answered, "Caesar's!" Jesus said, "Give to Caesar the things that belong to Caesar, and give to God the things that belong to God" (Matt. 22:15-22). His answer silence the so-called expert who sought to trap Him.

Another group came with a religious trick question. They said, "Moses told us that if a man dies without having children, his brother must marry the widow and raise up offspring for him. Now there were seven brothers among us. The first one married and died, and since he had no children, he left his wife to his brother. He married her and died with no children. All seven brothers married her one after the other and they all died. "At the resurrection whose wife this woman going to be?"

Jesus gave the answer that forever silence them on this matter. At the resurrection, she will be no one's wife, they will be like the angels of heaven, not married or given to marriage (Matt.22:23-33). The conflict between the religious elites of Judaism was palpable and culminated in a plot to murder Jesus.

Before Jesus allowed Himself to be taken, He exposed and denounced them repeatedly for their hypocrisy (Luke 11:17-54). And they hated Him the more. Eventually, Jesus condemned the whole rotten religious system. He prophesied its destruction and promised to replace it with something new (Matt.24:1-2).

The new worship system would not be Jerusalem centered or tied to a man-made building. It would not be dependent upon animal sacrifices (John 4:19-24). The religious elite led by the high priest, the chief priests, and most of the Sanhedrin, pushed back hard with a scheme to get rid of the Nazarene. This can be seen more clearly after the raising of Lazarus (John 11:45-53).

These powerful men who had gotten rich through the corrupted religious system were not willing to change, so they turned on the messenger and cleverly laid their traps to permanently silence Him by all necessary means. They played their hand well to advance a lie leading to the Messiah's execution and spawn a lying coverup of His resurrection that is still believed to this day among Jews (Matt.28:1-15).

Caiaphas, the high priest shouted the loudest to crucify Jesus, the seven chief priests shouted with him as well as the elders of the people and most of the Sanhedrin went along with the murderous plot as well (John 18:3, 12-14, 19-24, 19:1-7).

The irony is—from God's perspective, Jesus could have resisted arrest, destroyed the temple guards and the Romans with legions of angels (Matt.26:53-54). But instead of resisting them, He submitted to their authority and thereby fulfilled God's redemptive purpose (Isaiah 53:3-12).

Caiaphas was a shewed politician, a smooth operator, but from a Christian perspective, he was a spiritually blind man leading an elite club of blind men, and a nation that was mostly blind as well. The common people who followed Jesus had more spiritual insight than the gatekeepers of Israel who had the written revelation of God.

The blindness of the leaders was evident from the time of Jesus' birth. Angel announced the birth to shepherds on a Judean hillside. The angels said to them, "To you is born this day in the city of David, a Savior who is Christ the Lord?" (Luke 2:8-20). The shepherds closed their sheep pen and went in search of the child and found Him. They did not keep it quiet; they spread the news abroad. But dd the religious leaders investigate? No, they were too blind and too deaf to investigate.

Later, when the wise men arrived at king Herod's palace in the dead of night, asking for the newly born King of the Jews—Herod called for the elite priestly leaders of Israel. They went to his palace and provided the wicked king the information from their Scriptures where the child should be born. But they did not investigate; they went back to bed. Herod used that information to have his soldiers killed the children of Bethlehem two years of age and under in his effort to kill the Christ (Matt.2:1-23).

The God whom the priesthood represented stood before them in the person of Jesus Christ numerous times since His birth, and they failed to recognize Him. Why could they not recognize Him? Because they were spiritually blind and their religion badly corrupted. Let's look at this system more closely.

Summation

This chapter serves as the contextual overview in which Caiaphas, the high priest operated. Thus, the writer painted with broad strokes to show the power and influence Caiaphas had, as well as the cabinet of high priests, elders, and the mighty Sanhedrin. The next chapter will focus more closely on the high priest himself and each level of authority below him and in his circle of influence.

The power of the high priest had over the sacerdotal enterprise of the Hebrew nation at the time, can hardly be overstated. Only the Roman governor was over the high priest, politically speaking. The governor had the Roman legion to enforce his authority; less Jewish revolutionaries would have overthrown him at any time.

CHAPTER 2

PRIESTHOOD, ELDERS, AND THE TEMPLE

The priesthood and the Temple were central to the practice of Judaism during the time of Christ. The elders, though not clearly defined in the Scriptures, formed another influential group in Judaism. In this chapter, we will focus on the structure and function of the priesthood, say a little about the elders and the Temple. This is the context in which Caiaphas is to be understood with the added mix of Roman politics.

From the top down, the priesthood was made up of the high priest, the chief priests, the ordinary priests, and the Levites. Each level had its distinctive role. We have already stated that they all came from the tribe of Levi. All sacerdotal duties were remanded to the tribe of Levi by law.

But bear in mind that a tribe then was made up of many families. One prominent family of the tribe of Levi was the family of Aaron, the brother of Moses, and the first high priest. Aaron's four sons were priests but two sons (Nadab and Abihu died tragically when they "offered strange fire" (Lev.10: 1-12). Aaron's son Eleazer succeeded him as high priest.

God made it clear who could not become priest, even though he was of the lineage of Aaron. The Law states that the blind, lame, the disfigured, those with deformed limbs, broken hand or foot, hunchback or dwarf could not serve as priest. That includes anyone with blemishes or discoloration of the skin or any such conditions (Lev.21:16-23).

Healthy boys born to other families in the tribe of Levi, could work in the temple and in temple related jobs as Levites or by some other title. But they could not be priests. The priesthood was exclusive and selective as shown.

The Role the High Priest

The position of the high priest was unique in several ways, and his duties were extensive. We will only highlight a few of his most important duties in this chapter.

The high priest was the supreme representative and mediator between God and His people, as previously stated in chapter one. The office was most holy and of the highest significance above all others. The high priest carried the names of all twelve tribes over his heart, fixed in the breast piece of his garment. The office of high priest pointed to the Messiah; therefore, the high priest was a type of Christ, the heavenly high Priest that was to come.

But God knew in advance that the Aaronic Priesthood would have corrupted itself and come under the judgment of God. And For that reason, among others, the Priesthood of Christ is not after the Aaronic order but the order of Melchizedek which preceded the Aaronic order (Heb.7:11-11-16, 8:1-2). Jesus is not from the tribe of Levi but the tribe of Judah (Gen.49:10; Rev.5:5).

The High Priest Vestment. The *dignity* of the high priest's garment was unmistakably different. It was *designed* by God but made by humans. It had four parts: the breast piece, the ephod, the sash, and the turban. It also had a head covering.

It was designed to give the office of high priest *superior dignity* and set him apart from all else.[1] Just by seeing him, you would know that he was God's high priest, that he must be revered. And much more so, because the consecrated, anointing oil was upon him (Ex.28:1-30, 29:9; Lev.8:1-13; Psalm 133).

The High Priest had exclusive entry to the Mos Holy place. The high priest was the only one that could enter the immediate presence of God in the Most Holy place, and only on the Day of Atonement. There he would make intersession and atonement for the entire Nation. The very word *priesthood* in its root meaning points to one who "officiates" or "one who may draw near" to God (Ex.19:22, 30:20).[2]

Approval of Sacrificial Animals. There were certain offerings only the high priest could offer. For example, before he enters the Most Holy place, he offers the sin offering for himself and the congregation (Lev.4:3-12, 13-21). On the great Day of Atonement, he offers "the atoning sacrifice and the burnt offering" (Lev.16).[3]

The priests, including the high priest, would ensure that animals to be sacrificed conformed to the requirements of the Law before they were offered to God. Animals that were lame, blind, sick, or defective in anyway could not be offered to God because they would not be accepted. The high priest had supervision of all the other priest and all the sacerdotal matters. If it had to do with the worship of God, the high priest had the final say in the context of the Law.[4]

Another important function of the high priest was to inquiry of God on important matters facing the nation by means of the *Urim and the Thummim*(Num.27:21). These were two precious stones fixed in the breast piece of the high priest over his heart (Ex.28:30). The two words are said to mean, "light and perfection."[5] And may have changed color during inquiry to denote whether a thing was God's will or not. The high priest was the only one who had this authority.

King David, the anointed of God, used the priestly ephod to inquiry of God; that was an emergency exception (1Sam.30:7-8). The Hebrew priesthood evolved overtime and became more structured, professional, and even political, as we have seen with Caiaphas in chapter one.

The Chief Priests

The next level down from the high priest was the *chief priests*. The lay person often confuses high priest and the chief priests as if they were one and the same, but they are not. The term chief priests is most often written in the plural form which means more than one. By the time of Jesus ministry, there were seven chief priests, and they had to be all present for the giant doors of the Temple to be opened.[6]

Who were the chief priests? They occupy the prestigious and powerful position of regulating the activities of the Temple. They arranged and supervised the functions of the vast number of ordinary priests who perform the daily work for the smooth operation of the Temple.[7] Like the high priest, the chief priests were drawn from a small group of wealthy, powerful families with religious and political connections.[8] They had the resources to maintain their positions through bribery and nepotism.

They headed the elite class in Israel. Some hold on to power through conjugal bonds as with Annas and Caiaphas. That kept them circulating from one office of power to another. When they are not appointed as high priest, they serve as chief priests or regular member of the powerful Sanhedrin. So, they control the decision-making and policy-shaping of the nation, and the vast commerce and wealth of the Temple.

The Ordinary Priests

The ordinary priests was the third level down, the high priest being the first. The ordinary priests constituted most of the priesthood. By the time of Christ, there were over ten thousand ordinary priests. Most of them were poor and had to support themselves through means other than Temple duties.[9]

Some had trades as a means of support, some did farming, others had employment. The little they got from the ministry could not support their families, and at times they were even cheated out of that little they should have received from the ministry. Life was difficult for them.

Few ordinary priests lived in Jerusalem; they lived in various regions and cities and came to Jerusalem when it was their turn to serve in the temple, as well as during the three major feast days (Passover, Pentecost, and Atonement.[10]

Scholars observed that the vast number of ordinary priests were divided into twenty-four divisions, corresponding with specific priestly clans and served in the Temple on a rotational basis for one week twice each year.[11] So, if their year had fifty-two weeks like ours, fifty weeks were spent elsewhere. Of course, all the ordinary priests had to be on duty during the three major feast days as earlier indicated.

Vast crowds from all over the Roman empire would be in Jerusalem by law to celebrate the three major festivals as we see on the Day of Pentecost (Acts 2:1-8). All priestly hands would be needed for crowd control and other duties. So, at most an ordinary priest would make five trips *per annum* to Jerusalem.

The Levites

Levi was the third son of Jacob and Leah, for whom the Tribe of Levi was named (Genesis 29:34). On the one hand, therefore, the term "Levites" represent all the descendants of Levi (Ex.6: 25; Lev. 25:32; Jos.21:3,41). While on the other hand, Levites is the "distinct title for the portion of the tribe that was set apart for the service of the sanctuary and were subordinate to the priests" (Num.8:6; Ezra 2:70; John 1:19-20).[12]

Stated another way, priests were from the Aaronic lineage of the tribe of Levi, while the Levies were from other families within the tribe of Levi. Scholars assert that nearly "ten thousand men served the Temple as Levites on a rotation basis." Like the ordinary priest, they were organized into "twenty-four groups, each of which served one week twice each year."[13]

What were the duties of the Levites? Levites were Temple assistants; they did the heavy lifting. They carried out all the necessary tasks to keep the Temple operation orderly. For example, "Every evening, two hundred Levites were needed just to close the [massive] doors of the Temple."[14]

Levites served as Temple guards, they patrolled the grounds, they served as choirs, musicians; they did the bulk of the work. Their duties were varied and constant but performed according to their division or clan and assignment.[15]

In a Christian church setting, the Levites would be like the deacons, the choirs, musician, technicians, the janitorial staff, the security people, ushers, and the like. The Levites and the priest had distinct duties, but both were necessary for the function of the Temple. Without the Levites, the priests could not perform their duties, they all needed each other.

The Elders

In the nations of the ancient Near East, elders were the aged men who were the respected heads of families to whom the whole clan or nation looked to for wisdom and guidance (Deu.32:7-8; Job 12:12). Since books were not plentiful for record-keeping as they are today, the elders were keepers of the family's history and the larger clan, thus the development of the oral traditions, communicated by story-telling (Psalm 44:1-5).

The role of the elders. The elders were not exclusive to the Hebrew or Israelite people as already noted. But from the earliest of time, the elders among the Hebrews and Israelites served as priest of their families, judges, advisors of the clan, and they preserved the history, generally the oral history.

Men like Abraham, Isaac, Jacob were bearers of the covenant and became high valued elders. Many others with them were highly respected elders who held in trust the oral history of their people, and they were looked to for their wisdom, counsel, and guidance. From the earliest of time these functions were expected of elders by their people and by Yahweh himself.

For example, "God said of Abraham, 'For I chosen him, so that he will direct his children and his household after him to keep the way of the LORD by doing what is right and just, so that the LORD will bring about for Abraham what he has promised him'" (Gen.18:19). Abraham played the role of priest, guardian of the covenant, advisor, and defender for his family and clan. Abraham was called upon to defend the clan when his nephew and his family were taken captives.

Sodom was besieged and overrun by a coalition of ten kings and Lot, Abraham's nephew, was taken captive, the clan looked to Abraham for guidance and strategic action. Abraham provided such leadership and was victorious, defeating the enemy and recovered Lot and his family. The hand of Yahweh is evident in this victory; it is marked in the celebration that followed with Melchizedek (Gen.14:13-24).

So, the term elders, among the Hebrews, predated the Levitical priesthood which was put in place during the *Wilderness Journey* at Sinai by Moses. Before Moses arrived in Egypt to demand the release of his people, Yahweh directed him to first present the plan to the elders of the people, to secure their cooperation. Moses should have them accompany him meeting with Pharoh, king of Egypt (Ex.3:16-18, 4:29). The stakes could not be higher. So, with the commitment of the elders, the people could have confidence that this liberation move was not some half-baked scheme of a man missing for forty years.

In Exodus 12:21, Moses summoned, the elders of Israel to a meeting in which he briefed them concerning the celebration of the first Passover and commissioned them to "Go at once and select the animals for your families and slaughter the Passover lamb." Again, why the elders? They were the respected authorities who served as priests, judges, and advisers to their families and the larger clans.

Much is not said about the elders again until Moses' father-in-law, Jethro, came to visit Moses and the elders were invited to sacrifice and break bread with him (Ex.18:12).

The wise Jethro observed that Moses was over-worked, sitting as judge from morning to evening hearing the cases of his people, while capable men like the elders, were sitting there doing nothing. Jethro counseled Moses to appoint these capable, honest, and respectable men as judges over thousands, hundreds, and tens to hear the less complicated cases, while Moses hears the more complex cases. This way the congregation shared the workload, and the people went home early (Ex.18:13-27).

There is no doubt that God approved because Moses adopted and implemented all Jethro's advice (verses 24-26). Jethro's shared approach to leadership was superior to Moses' singular model. Superior in the sense that it took the burden off one person and distributed it more broadly. It gave opportunity and responsibility to others to serve and exercise their skills. It got more done in a shorter period, and it prevented burnout.

By adopting Jethro's recommendation, Moses revealed his own character of humility and graciousness. Pride would have prevented some leaders from submitting to the fatherly advice and wisdom of their fathers-in-law. Moses welcome the advice.

Later, Moses reflected on how the heavy burden of leadership impacted him, and how he adopted Jethro's wise counsel that he first presented to God (Deu.1:9-19).

Sharing leadership responsibility with the elders in no way diminished Moses' leadership; it enhanced it. He later gave his "communications and commands from God through the elders to the people" (Ex.19:7-9). Finally, Moses' farewell charge was not only given to Joshua and the priests, but also to the elders of the people (Deu.31:9).

The elders during the time of Christ. Though not a clearly defined group in the gospels, by the time of Jesus' ministry, the elders evolved to be an influential group, shaping the politics and religion of the nation.

Scholars believe some of them were wealthy landowners, businessmen who served on the Sanhedrin where policies were made and implemented. They were men like Nicodemus and Joseph of Arimathea. They were part of "the Jewish aristocracy and nobility."[16]

The elders were the ones who shaped the tradition governing Jewish life. Tradition sometimes overruled the text of scripture. The authorities once accused the disciples Jesus for not following the tradition of the elders. Jesus pointed out to them that they break the commands of God for the sake of their tradition (Matt.15:1-2).

The elders also served as leaders in various towns and cities. They were advisers to kings, priest, and governors "on important matters facing the nation."[17]

Matthew does not say much about the elders as a distinct group in the earlier part of Jesus ministry. Jesus' conflict was always with the Scribes and Pharisees, and minimally with the Sadducees. Some of these same men may have been elders. But with the cleansing of the Temple, two groups questioned Jesus as to his authority to do what he did; they were the chief priests and the elders (Matt.21:23-27).

However, in their attempt to formulate a plot to kill Jesus, three power groups are mentioned: the chief priests, the scribes, and the elders. They had a meeting at the palace of the high priest (Matt.26:1-5 NKJV). These are the power people, the elite, the policy makers of Judaism.

Matthew again named the chief priests and elders as the ones authorizing the arrest of Jesus; some were physically present when it was executed (verse 47), while others were waiting at the palace Caiaphas, the high priest, where the scribes, elders of the people were assembled, undoubtedly the full Sanhedrin (Matt.26: 57-59).

"All the chief priests and elders of the people" not only tried Jesus illegally and condemned him to death, but the next morning also they brought him to the Roman governor to rubber stamp his condemnation for the execution (Matt.27:1-2).

The chief priests and elders accused Jesus before the governor (verses 11-12, 20-23). The elders were also among those who mocked Jesus while he was dying on the cross (verses 41-43). The same groups that conspired to kill Jesus (chief priests, scribes, and elders) now engaged in a bribery scheme to payoff of the soldiers to coverup the resurrection of the Christ (Matt.28:11-15).

The gospel of Mark has fewer mention of the elders as a group than Matthew. But like Matthew, the first mention of them is in connection with Jesus' authority to cleanse the Temple (Mark 11:27). Mark does not mention the bribe paid to the soldiers in the attempt to coverup the resurrection of the Christ.

Luke agrees with Matthew and Mark but mentioned the elders as a group fewer time than Mark. Of the three synoptic gospels, Matthew uses the term *elder* most frequently.

John's gospel hardly speak of the elders as separate group. Where the synoptic gospels used the term elders to designate a separate group, John does not. Instead, chief priests, scribes, and pharisees are used. This confirms that this word "elders" was used interchangeably with those groups. The prior conclusion therefore stands that they were largely respected men of wealthy and influence to whom the nation looked for guidance.

The Temple

The centrality of the Temple in Jewish life up to the first century A.D. can hardly be exaggerated. It was a Levitical institution as already shown. We will just say a little about the structure itself in this chapter and discuss its history and administration in another chapter.

The Temple was not a single building, but a complex with several buildings enjoined to serve the sacerdotal, health, and even commerce to some extent. Buying and selling went on in the courts of the Temple and some of it was necessary, but it got out of hand, thus resulting in its cleansing by Jesus the Christ.

While there were many synagogues throughout the Roman empire where Jews lived for regular worship, scripture reading, and education, there was only one Temple. It was in Jerusalem on Mount Moriah, the place where Abraham was tested to offer his son, Isaac as a sacrifice to God (Gen.22:1-19). But God provided a ram to take Isaac's place.

The first Temple was built there by King Solomon, but was later destroyed in 586 B.C. by Nebuchadnezzar, king of Babylon because Israel had forsaken God (Jeremiah 52). After seventy years, the Temple was rebuilt by decree of King Cyrus of Persia. Cyrus provided the people (Jews) and the financing of the project. The people contributed willingly as well (Ezra 1:1-11).

So, a remnant of Jews returned from Babylon (now Persia because Babylon had fallen), led by the prophet Ezra (3:7-13). Ezra was also called Zerubbabel (4:1-5). The rebuilt house of the Lord was called, the Zerubbabel's Temple. It was inferior in grandeur and magnificence to the previous Temple built by Solomon. It suffered significant damage over time but was not completely destroyed.

By the time of Jesus, a new Temple complex was built on the same cite without destroying the older structure. This was significantly larger and more magnificent in grandeur. It was built as a gift to the Jews by Herod the Great. Some said it took forty-six years to build but others say, it took over eighty years (John 2:18-21).[18] This imposing structure was the pride of Israel and the seat of first century Judaism. It was controlled by the priesthood; they were its administrators and gatekeepers.

The Temple was a multiplex: a place of worship and sacrifice, judicial proceedings, education, health certification, commerce, and law enforcement. It was given a high level of autonomy to operate in cooperation with Rome. The high priest was at the head of this powerful institution with the support of the Sanhedrin. Below the high priest were the seven chief priests who form a type of cabinet. They wield great powers.

Below the chief priests situated nearly "ten thousand ordinary priests,"[19] and below them about "ten thousand Levites."[20] The elders were not as clearly defined as the priesthood and perhaps included the high and chief priests. They were a group of wealthy men, highly respected and influential. They helped to shape the traditions of the Israel and form policies; some had seats on the Sanhedrin.

This chapter gives you a broad view of the Levitical priesthood and the Temple during the time of Christ, first century AD. The ministry of Jesus impacted and changed Judaism for all times. The point of impact was the fact that Jesus came as Israel's Messiah, God incarnate, to redeem His people and the world, but the priesthood, the religious elite and leaders of the people did not recognize Him as such. Next, we will look at the administration of the Temple.

CHAPTER 3

THE TEMPLE ADMINISTRATION

The center of the Levitical sacerdotal system was the priesthood and the Temple; like head and neck, one could hardly function without the other. The system was complex yet highly structured. It had a well-structured building, a structured labor force; the function of each person was clearly defined.

The system was thoroughly legalistic; it had powers and authority over Jewish life throughout the Roman empire. But it was somewhat restricted because it could not try and execute a Roman citizen. That was the prerogative of the Roman governor.

An understanding of accommodation and cooperation was reached between Rome and Israel. So, the people of Israel were allowed to practice their religion, conduct commerce, and enforce their own laws with certain minimal restrictions.

As already stated, the death penalty for civil crimes was the prerogative of the Roman governor. Israel was not given that power. That was one reason Caiaphas did not carry out the execution of Jesus himself. He wanted Pilate to do it. But he needed a civil charge to bring Jesus to Pilate. The charge he produced was treason. Jesus claimed to be king, but "we have no king but Caesar" (Matt.27:1-2, 11-18; John 18:28-38).

However, at times overzealous religious fanatic would stone people to death as they did Stephen, and without consequences from the civil authorities (Acts 7:1, 54-60). The governor would not normally be judge on Jewish religious matters, nor would Jewish religious leaders judge civil crimes.

The Temple was the central place of operation for the Levitical system. The work force spoken of in Chapter 2 from high priest to Levites, largely carried out their professional and assigned duties in the context of the Temple, and under its authorization and supervision. Saul of Tarsus obtained arrest warrants from the high priest to bring Jewish followers of Jesus from other cities to Jerusalem for trial (Acts 9:1-6). The administrators of the Temple had certain judicial powers over Jews everywhere.

There was one Temple, situated in Jerusalem. It was the place where the Ark of the Covenant rested and the only place that sacrifices could be offered. There were synagogues in many cities for sabbath worship and education. Bu the major festivals, like Passover, Day of Atonement, and Pentecost, were held in Jerusalem at the Temple and by law Jews everywhere had to attend (Acts 2:1-11). Again, the priests and Levites were fully in charge of the administration of the Temple by Jewish law.

A Brief History of the Temple

THE TEMPLE ADMINISTRATION

The first public house of worship for the Israelites was the Tabernacle, a portable tent used during the Exodus. God gave Moses the architectural plans and its furnishing on Mount Sinai. It was also called The Tent of Meeting. It was built by men chosen by God; they carefully followed the patterns shown to Moses on the mountain (Ex.25:1-8, 33: 7-11).

The people provided the material, the offering to the pay the workmen, and the labor. It was the house of God but each person was a stake holder and so they contributed to the cost. The Tabernacle served their individual and collective needs. They traveled with this Tent of Meeting (Ex.35:4-29).

The first stationary place of worship was Solomon's Temple, built in Jerusalem on Mount Mariah. The was the project of King David. But God did not allow him to build it because he was a man of war whose hands had shed blood. God commended David for wanting to honor Him in this. But he told him his son Solomon would build the Temple instead (2 Chron.1-2).

Nonetheless, David prepared the plans after the pattern of the Tabernacle and provided materials and financing for the construction. But his son King Solomon was the one to build and dedicate the Temple to the glory of God (2 Chron. 5-7).

It was a most magnificent and awe-inspiring structure and God was pleased with it. Solomon had spared no expenses building the Temple. The interior was lavishly overlaid with gold. But it was not the man-made building God was interested in; He was interested in His covenant people Israel. Without their *exercise of faith and obedience*, the building meant nothing to God. Faith and obedience was the glue of the covenant.

CAIAPHAS The Pernicious High Priest

When Israel persistently turned away from the true God to serve idols, they violated the covenant that tied them to Yahweh. So, they were delivered into the hands of Nebuchadnezzar, king of Babylon. His army came and besieged Jerusalem, knocked down its walls, destroyed the Temple, and carried off the most vibrant and talented of its people to Babylon. (Jer.52). This was the curse of the covenant being released on a faithless and disobedient people (see Deu.28:15-68).

After seventy years of exile in Babylon, a remnant was allowed to return to rebuild the Temple under Ezra and the walls of Jerusalem under Nehemiah. The rebuilt Temple was inferior to the previous Temple of Solomon. This caused rejoicing and weeping from the laying of its foundation (Ezra 3:12-13).

By the time of Jesus, a new Temple was built with its supporting building, larger and more imposing than previous ones. It was built by one of the Herod's as a gift to the Jews; it took forty-six years to complete; some sources say over eighty. It was really the pride and joy of Israel. But by this time, Israel was under Roman occupation. Just above this Temple site was Fort Antonio where the Roman soldiers were stationed.

By this time Judaism had become extremely corrupted. The office of high priest was a political appointment; it was given to the most influential bidder who was wealthy and could afford the bribe to the governor. The administration of the Temple was in the hands of wealthy elites.

Caiaphas the high priest and seven chief priests were at the very pinnacle of the Temple administration. The other elite member had a seat on the Chief Council called the Sanhedrin. It had seventy men plus the chairman, the high priest. Their positions made them increasingly rich. But that wealth was not filtered down to the nearly ten thousand ordinary priests, and over ten thousand Levites who did most of the work.

Yet, the Temple was a cash cow. Temple tax, fees, and offerings from tens of thousands of people constantly flow through its coffers and treasury, especially upon festivals days. The Temple was highly commercialized; it even had its own currency.[1] Nothing corrupts more than power and money in the hands of greedy, sinful men. And that's exactly what happened.

The unrighteous mammon had taken over and repurpose the house of God from a house of worship and prayer to den of thieves and made the religious leaders corrupted and conniving and Caiaphas presided over it. All this placed them and the entire Temple operation on a collision course with Jesus, the Christ.

Jesus and the Temple

Apart from the office of the prophet, the Levitical priesthood had charge of the entire sacerdotal system for the nation (Israel).[2] They were the custodians, interpreters, teachers, and enforcers of the of Law of God and the traditions of the elders They were the keepers of Ark of the Covenant, the administrators, and guardians of the Temple. They carried it out to the letter, but they were corrupted, greedy, and without mercy and compassion.

By the time of Jesus' public ministry, Judaism had amassed a significant body of written practices called, the oral Law or tradition of the elders. This was expert interpretation of the written Law overtime, equivalent to legal precedence in our time. They were given equal status to the written Law and in some cases superseded the written Law. Jesus rebuked the Scribes and Pharisees over these practices (Matt.15:1-13).

Additionally, Judaism had divided itself into sects such as Pharisees, Scribes, Sadducees, and Elders as observed in all four gospels There was also a splinter group known as the Essenes.[1] Some say John the Baptist was an Essene.

Bear in mind that Jesus was and is the supreme and perfect fulfillment of the Law of God that was handed down through Moses. The Law covered all aspects of life—human and divine relationships: worship, family life, health, property, money and commerce, employer and worker, human sexuality, treatment of the poor, and how to treat the stranger. The priesthood which was established by that same set of laws was made custodians and enforcers of the Law (Deuteronomy 31:9-13; Joshua1:8-9). That was a lot of power in the hands of a few, but God expected righteousness, justice, and mercy of them (Micah 6:8).

Jesus started His ministry by ratifying the Law in his Sermon on the Mount (Matt.5-7). Jesus did not abolish the Law (5:17-20). Note the process of this ratification in the frequent use of the expression, "It was said, but I say" (Matt.5:21, 27, 31-43). Jesus was not only giving the correct interpretation of the written Law; He was overruling some of the traditions of the elders and establishing new precedence. What Christians refer to as the Old Testament, remains the Word of God and must be understood in Jesus Christ. He is the fullness of the Word of God.

The Sermon on the Mount, therefore, forms the foundation of Jesus' ministry of teaching and preaching. In His explanation of the Scripture, Jesus put Himself in direct conflict with the religious elites of Scribes and pharisees. They considered themselves the authority on Scripture and over Jewish life.

They thought they knew the Word of God better than this unlettered rabbi, this self-proclaimed Messiah from Nazareth as they called Him (John 7:14). The irony is, Jesus was and is the personified Word of God (John 1:1-2,14; Rev.19:11-16). He expounded the Scriptures about Himself beginning with the writings of Moses (the Torah), then the prophets; they all wrote of Him (Luke 24:13-35).

The Scribes and Pharisees placed tremendous emphasis on external purity: ritual washings, sabbath observance, and their biological connect to Abraham. By doing all that they sincerely thought they were, guaranteed a place in the kingdom of God.

But on the other hand, Jesus emphasized inner purity, love, justice, mercy, forgiveness, faith, and obedience to the Word of God. These were more important to God than family connection to Abraham. God was looking for faith and obedience; He was looking for people who were won inwardly (John 8:13-47).

The religious elite accused Jesus of being an imposter, demon possessed, and a blasphemer whose behavior would put them in conflict with the Romans and cause them to lose their Temple and comfortable accommodation with Rome.

The commerce of the Temple had made these men wealthy and powerful, and Jesus was now a threat to that commerce.[3] With that they pushed back hard against Jesus, endeavoring to maintain the status quo of a corrupted system rather than yield to the message of repentance that Jesus was preaching.

Another irony was that Jesus, their long-awaited Messiah, was walking among them, and they were totally blind to that revelation. It reveals the depth to their spiritual condition; they were spiritually lost, and it was for this reason Jesus came "to seek and to save that which was lost" (Matt.18:11). But they did not understand the concept of spiritual blindness and lostness.

It is most difficult to save a drowning man who does not know he is drowning or to redirect a lost person who does not know he is lost or to convince a health man that he needs a physician. When Jesus described their spiritual condition using these terms, they said, "We are Abraham children, we have never been in bondage to anyone" (John 8:32-33). We are the chosen of God; we are fine. This was the superior attitude of the religious elite. They could not see Him in their own Scriptures.

They were oblivious to the fact that they were corrupted and were presiding over a corrupted religious system that they vociferously guarded. Jesus did not come to maintain that corrupted system but to change it by offering salvation first to Israel, then to the rest of the world (John 3:16). But they steadfastly rejected Him and all that He stood for (John 1:12). With that they set out to trap and kill Him.

Religious people are most dangerous when they are convinced that they are acting for God. The high priest, the chief priests, the elders, and most members of the Sanhedrin were convinced they were the true defenders of the faith, and they were doing God's bidding. They did not care whether the one they entrapped and killed was guilty or innocent. The high priest said, it was better that one man die for the nation than the whole nation perish (John 18:14). These were the men who served as administrators of the Temple institution, headed by Caiaphas.

CHAPTER 4

CAIAPHAS THE HUNTER

"Then...Caiaphas...spoke up, 'You know nothing at all! You do not realize that it is better for you that one man die for the people than the whole nation perish'" (John 11:49-50).

The *high priest* Caiaphas was the highest religious authority and most decorated personality in all of Israel. The Roman governor was the highest political authority.

It was God Himself who specified the design of the regalia or vestments the *high priest* wore. His dignity, function, and authority was above all other Levitical offices. He was God's representative to the nation and the nation's representative before God. This was most vividly portrayed on the Day of Atonement as he entered the Most Holy Place to make intersession before God for the nation. But when God's interest is superseded by self-interest, the man and the office became corrupted. And so it was with Caiaphas, the high priest.

This holy man was so offended by Jesus of Nazareth, that he set out to have him followed around to find cause for his arrest. They charged Him for healing on the sabbath day and cited his disciple for breaking corn on the sabbath day and for eating with ceremonially unwashed hands. Jesus showed them from scripture that He and His disciple were acting in compliance with the Law (Matt.12:1-12).

Caiaphas and his group sent out experts in the Law to trap Jesus at every turn. They asked questions such as "who is my neighbor? Whose wife will a woman be at the resurrection if she married multiple times? Is it lawful to pay taxes to Ceasar?" (Matt.22:15-33). Jesus answered their questions from the Scriptures correctly, that even those sent to arrest Him returned without Him saying, "Never a man spoke like this man," "he taught as one having authority" (Mark 1:22).

Jesus knew the religious leaders wanted to kill Him, and from time to time, He exposed their corrupted intent in His teachings. Rather than repenting of their malevolence, they became even more determined to take His life (Luke 4:28-29

The feeling that an unschooled teacher from a peasant village like Nazareth could have a better understanding of the Law and commanded more followers was humiliating to the elite leaders. And it stirred them to jealousy and murder. Like an autopsy, this book reveals the spiritual malignancy of their campaign to silence the Nazarene (Matt.26:1-5).

Blind religiosity is dangerous and cruel. Saul of Tarsus was a sincere defender of his Jewish faith; he thought he was acting for God when he hunted down Christians and brough them in chains to Jerusalem to stand trial (Acts 9:1-5). Saul thought he was doing God's service persecuting followers of Christ. Saul was cut from the same religious cloth as Caiaphas.

But unlike Saul, Caiaphas and the chief priests and elders who set out to trap and kill Jesus knew they were breaking their own Law to kill Jesus. They sought false witnesses to testify against Jesus. They arrested and tried him at night which was unlawful. They knew they were setting out to shed innocent blood (Matt.26:14-67). They said, "His blood is on us and on our children" (Matt. 27:20-26). But they did not care if the curse of shedding innocent blood were credited to their children and grandchildren. Even the mafia would not say such a thing because they are family-minded people.

But not all members of the Sanhedrin agreed to the murderous plot directed against Jesus. Jesus was not only popular among the common people, but he also had a few secret supporters on the Council. For example, Nicodemus who visited Jesus by night and Joseph of Arimathea who later asked the governor to release the body of Jesus and gave it a decent burial. These two men were secret followers of Jesus who had seats on the Sanhedrin and voted, no to the plot to kill Jesus.

Jesus also had the support of some prominent women who were married to influential men. In fact, the governor's wife was one such woman, and she warned her husband about doing right by this just man (Matt. 27:19). The Roman governor had no prior ill will toward Jesus of Nazareth. In fact, he found Him innocent of all charges and wanted to let Him go. But the religious elite vehemently objected to the point of threatening the governor's position (Verse 20).

Caiaphas, the chief priests, the elders, and others who had seats on the Sanhedrin were politically savvy men who could influence Rome to have Ceasar recall the governor.[1] The governor was fully aware of this underhanded leverage that Caiaphas and his group had and so he capitulated to their demands. For political expediency, Pilate rubber-stamped the crucifixion of Jesus, even though he knew the Nazarene was innocent; he said so at least three times (John 18:38-40, 19:17).

Heretofore, Jesus escaped from all the plots against His life because His hour was not yet come. In the economy of God, Jesus could not die before the time God ordained for him to die for the redemption of humankind (Gal. 4:4-6). His death was calculated to the very day and hour.

For that reason, Jesus always said my time is not yet come. Or "No man takes my life from me; I have power to lay it down and power to pick it up again" (John 10:17-18). Or "Destroy this temple and I will raise it up in three days" (John 2:18-22). By that He meant that He would be resurrected three days after His death, and that was the way it happened indeed.

The raising of Lazarus commenced the first full-fledged plot launched against the life of Jesus Christ. Yes, several attempts were made before, from His hometown synagogue to the Temple in Jerusalem. But now the threat on His life was entrenched; He could hardly walk openly in Judea. That was the reason for Thomas' skeptical comment about going back to that area (John 11:14-16). In substance, Thomas was saying, all of us may very well end up dead, not just Lazarus.

Jesus had a close friendship with Lazarus and his two sisters, Mary, and Martha (John 11:1-44). They lived in Bethany, less than two miles from Jerusalem (verse 18). Jesus would normally stay with this family when He was in town.

The sisters sent to call Jesus when their brother took ill, but Jesus did not go immediately in response to the urgent call to come and heal their brother. Jesus delayed going for two days (verses 4-7). And by the time He arrived, Lazarus had been dead and buried for four days (verse 17). This delay was not by chance but by design; Jesus planned it that way.

He intended to use the raising of Lazarus to demonstrate to unbelieving Israel that He was the Messiah, the Son of God. Before this, some religious authorities denied the authenticity of his healing and exorcism by crediting them to Satan. So, Lazarus had to be unquestionably dead so no one could deny it.

Jewish tradition holds that the spirit of the dead lingers near the body for three days then departs to Sheol when decay starts.[2] Lazarus, being dead four days and buried, no one could deny that an authentic miracle had taken place to bring him back to life. Satan cannot bring anyone back to life; therefore, the intervention of God cannot be denied. Jesus wanted all Israel to know He has power over life and death (verses 41-42).

"Jesus wept" (verse 35). But again, His weeping was not just because He was grieving for Lazarus and his sisters. He was weeping for all unbelieving Israel. For He knew that despite this miracle, Israel would not accept Him as their Messiah. Many of the Jews who had come to support Mary and Martha and witnessed what had taken place were now convinced that Jesus was indeed the Messiah (verse 45).

But others did not believe in Jesus, despite such a spectacular miracle. The unbelievers immediately reported the miracle to the religious authorities in Jerusalem. And did they glorify God for what He was doing among them? No! they became outraged and indignant against Jesus. Caiaphas, the high priest, immediately convened an emergency meeting of the Sanhedrin to put a stop to this Jesus of Nazareth (John 11:47).

The Sanhedrin Meets

The head religious authority in all of Israel at this time was Caiaphas, the high priest. He and the chief priests below him considered the raising of Lazarus such an earthshaking event, it warranted an emergency session of this High Council, not to consider the question that this man Jesus may very well be the long-awaited Messiah of Israel. Neither was the meeting to pray and search the Scriptures for guidance. Why? They had already concluded that Jesus was not the Messiah but an imposter and a blasphemer. And it was high time that the Council did something about it. Here is the discussion of the Council:

> What are we accomplishing? they asked. Here is the man performing many signs. If we let him go on like this, everyone will believe in him, and then the Romans will come and take away both our temple and our nation.
> Then one of them named Caiaphas, who was high priest that year, spoke up, 'You know nothing at all! You do not realize that it is better for you that one man die for the people than the whole nation perish.'... So then from that day on they plotted to take his life.

Therefore, Jesus no longer moved about publicly among the people of Judea. Instead, he withdrew to the region near the wilderness, to a village called Ephraim, where he stayed with his disciples (John 11:47-54).

The Council concluded with an executive order that anyone knowing the whereabouts of Jesus should report it to the authorities and they will come and arrest him (Verse 57). The Council cast a wide net to arrest Jesus and have Him killed; this was the plot. But why, why were they so afraid of Jesus?

The contents of the preceding, lengthy quotation from the Sanhedrin provides the answer. *First*, they acknowledge that their previous efforts to trap Jesus were not successful. *Second*, they were afraid that everyone would believe in Him if they did not stop him now. *Third*, they were afraid that the Romans would come and take away their Temple and the whole nation (verse 48). Their comfortable living would be forever gone.

They were willing to kill Jesus to keep their Temple, preserve their lucrative way of life, and continue their corrupted practices. They thought getting rid of Jesus guaranteed the longevity of the Temple and national safety with the Romans.

But the very thing they feared would be the thing that would happen later. They ended up losing the Temple and their nation, not because of the ministry of Jesus but due to their own unbelief that set them on this murderous trajectory against the Nazarene.

The Palm Sunday Procession

Despite an active warrant out for His arrest, Jesus was back at Bethany. According to John's account, six days before the Passover Jesus arrived in Bethany; that is the Saturday evening after the sabbath. A dinner was given in His honor at Lazarus's house. It was at this time Mary, one of Lazarus' sisters, poured an expensive ointment on the feet of Jesus (John 12:1-8).

But Judas objected, classifying it as a waste; that it could have been sold and the money given to the poor. Jesus rebuked Judas by coming to the Mary's defense (verses 7-8).

The news spread quickly that Jesus was back in the area, and a crowd gathered outside to see both Jesus and Lazarus. By this time news also reached the religious authorities, and the chief priests made plans to kill Lazarus as well (John 12:9-10).

The next day, Sunday, the beginning of Passover week, Jesus arrived in Jerusalem at the center of procession: a large crowd leading and a large crowd following (Matt.21:8-9). He was riding a borrowed donkey and welcomed and cheered by a jubilant, palm waving crowd. They shouted, "Hosanna! Blessed is he who comes in the name of the Lord! Blessed is the king of Israel" (John 12:12-13).

Jesus did not declare Himself as king, others wanted to make Him king after the feeding of the five thousand. He had to escape from them making Him king by force (John 6:13-15). Again, the crowds are at it. But now they see Him as the Son of David, the king that the prophets said should come and reign on David's throne (Isaiah 9: 6-7). They got the person right but the timing wrong, because Jesus' mission at this time was not to sit on any earthly throne but to give His life a ransom for many (Matt. 20:28). He came to inaugurate the New Covenant (Jer.31:31-37).

Riding into Jerusalem on a donkey was also the fulfillment of Zachariah's prophecy (9:9):which says:

> Tell the daughters of Zion,
> Behold, your King is coming to you,
> Lowly, and sitting on a donkey,
> A colt, the foal of a donkey. (Zech.9:9)

This triumphant entry to Jerusalem was no small matter. Matthew gives us this intelligence report: "And when He was come into Jerusalem, all the city was moved, saying, 'Who is this?' So, the multitudes said, 'This is Jesus, the prophet from Nazareth of Galilee'"(Matt.21:9 NKJV).

The religious authorities immediately knew the significance of the message Jesus was communicating. By entering the city not on a war horse but on a donkey was a symbol of peace. To them, Jesus was saying, I am the Messiah, the King of whom the prophets spoke. If that is the case, then our worst nightmare has come true. The Romans will see consider this provocative and will come and destroy our Temple, our city, and our nation.

The fact is—the Hebrew Bible's religious symbol of a preacher riding a donkey to town would have had no meaning to the Romans. Therefore, if the religious leaders had embraced Jesus as their Messiah, the fear of losing their Temple would not have materialized. The ride into Jerusalem should have given pause to the religious elite to back away from their murderous campaign against Jesus. But it strengthened their resolve to kill Him instead.

The Cleansing of the Temple

The synoptic gospels (Matthew, Mark, and Luke) show that the procession went directly to the Temple. The praise and worship with the common people, went from the street to the Temple, where commerce was in full swing for Passover.

The Temple was the stronghold of the priesthood, the religious elite, the elders, the Sanhedrin. This was what they lived for, and they would defend it to their last breath. They were the administrators, controllers, and defenders of this place. They think they were doing it for God, but it had become corrupted under their watch, and they showed no willingness to clean it up.

Now, suddenly the Lord is in His Holy Temple and He is not pleased with what they have done to His house. He shows that space is not the property of the religious elite. It is the house of God, a place of prayer for all people. They have corrupted and reduced this sacred space to a marketplace.

With that declaration that they have made the house of God a marketplace and they have become a den of thieves, Jesus began to drive them out. He overturned the tables of the money-changers and those that sold does and other merchandise (Matt. 21:12-13). This was now pandemonium.

Jesus acted as one having authority, but the high priest, chief priests, elders, and members of the Sanhedrin considered themselves the true authority, not this self-proclaimed messiah from the peasant village of Nazareth. He is an imposter! That was their line of thinking. They were spiritually blind.

Now bear in mind that most of this merchandising was not in the sanctuary proper, but in the Temple court. And some business transactions were necessary. Jesus understood all that; there is no knowledge deficit on His part concerning these matters. From infancy, He had been making trips to the Temple; he had to be carried back then (Luke 2:22-40).

Thousands of people came from different regions of the Roman empire to celebrate the festival of Passover. It was too cumbersome to bring animals for sacrifice over such great distance. Instead, they brought money and purchased the animals in Jerusalem, even at the Temple court. That was most convenient. But it reduced their buying options and made them more vulnerable to the overcharge of greedy merchants.

Temple court merchants had to pay a fee for their spot, and this was not void of nepotism and bribery. They were in business for a profit. That made the competition fierce, aggressive, loud!

Furthermore, there was not a uniform currency such as the United States has today, that is good in all fifty States. Different regions had their own currency, even the Temple had its own currency.* To transact business with the Temple, a person had to convert the currency he was holding to the Temple currency. That was one reason, among others, for the money-changers. They provided a needed service for a fee.

The money-changers' fee was competitive with the other merchants. Therefore, to get the attention of customers, the merchants must attract them with a little shouting. Several merchants leaving their stalls or calling from their stalls would indeed make the place a lively marketplace. The sounds and smell of animals also added a unique flavor to the mix.

The manner they were conducting themselves in addition to overcharging people, reduced the house of God to something less than that for which it was intended. And since the gate-keepers did not intend to do anything about it, the true Master of the House, the Lord Himself, had to deploy corrective measures.

Again, Jesus was not out of touch with all this commotion; He had been watching this misuse of the Temple all His life. He had been coming to Jerusalem for these festivals since He was twelve years of age, and from that time the Temple was considered His Father's business (Luke 2:41-52). But at that age, His time was not yet come to change the system. This final Passover was His scheduled time to die and inaugurate the new covenant. His time had come to act decisively, and He did.

Response to the Cleansing of the Temple

As stated earlier, the gate-keepers to the Temple and its ministry were the priesthood, the Levites, the elders of the people, and the Sanhedrin; they were indignant to the actions of Jesus. Jesus did not just disperse the buying and selling crowd, He replace them with his Hosana crowd including children, and people with health needs to whom he ministered (Matt.21:14-16).

The next day, Jesus returned to the Temple courts and ministered to the people. The gate-keepers confronted Him and asked, "By what authority are you doing these things?" "And who gave him this authority?" (verse 23). This is a clever or trick question, because in their minds, they are the authority and that authority came directly from God, and none of them had given authority to Jesus of Nazareth to disrupt the activities of the Temple. Jesus knew this is a trick question intended to trap Him.

Jesus responded, I will ask you one question. If you answer me, I will tell you by what authority I do these things. John the Baptist's baptism was it from heaven or of men? This question was also a trick question. Because if they answer that John got his authority from heaven to baptize, Jesus would have asked, Why then did you not obey John? If they said, John got his authority from men, the people would have stoned them, for they all regarded John as a prophet from God. The gate-keepers answered that they did not know where John got his authority. Jesus answered, "Neither will I tell you where I get my authority" (Matt.21:23-27). This harden their resolve to kill Jesus (Mark 11:18).

The Hunt is On

From the raising of Lazarus, the religious authorities were determined to kill Jesus and so they issued a warrant for His arrest (John 11:45-54). The procession into Jerusalem on Palm Sunday, and the cleansing of the Temple provoked a more urgent crusade to get rid of Jesus. To the religious leaders, these actions of Jesus were dangerous and deserved the penalty of death.

But there were two barriers. On the one hand, Jesus was popular with the common people and any attempt to take Him publicly may spark a riot, thus making things worse for the religious leaders. On the other hand, God was at work in the matter, but these gatekeepers did not recognize His hand. God's plan was for Jesus to die on Passover, not before, not after.

Let it be clear, the hand of God in the death of His Son does not justify or nullify the wickedness of the gatekeepers. It was not God causing them to do what they did. They got their inspiration from their own sinful nature, and from the same evil spirit that entered Judas (Luke 22:1-6).

Jesus did not need help to lay down His life redemptively. That He could do without their wicked hands and conniving hearts of Caiaphas and his group. As they plotted how to take Jesus by subtility and kill Him, Satan informed them that he had an insider on the ministry team of Jesus that could be of immense help them. Satan prodded Judas to go to the religious leaders.

Satan had been prepping Judas for this hour of opportunity for some time. Matthew writes, "Then one of the twelve, called Judas Iscariot, went to the chief priests and said, 'What are you willing to give to me if I deliver Him to you?' And they counted out to him thirty pieces of silver. So, from that time he sought opportunity how he might betray Him" (Matt.26:14-16 NKJV).

Judas volunteered to deliver the package for a price, and for that job he was paid in full for the delivery. How did Judas pull this devilish scheme off? He first sold out to Satan. He kept his dirty secret to himself, but Jesus knew what he was up to and exposed Judas' big, devilish secret the other disciples. They were dumbfounded (John 13:25-30).

Judas had his feet washed but his heart was dirty (verse 10-12). He excused himself from the Last Supper table to finalize his betrayal deal (verse 30). Like Cain, Judas left worship to commit murder; they were both backslidden in heart as well as spiritual brothers (Gen. 4:3-8; 1John 3:10-12).

Judas absent himself from the Gethsemane prayer meeting to do the devil's work. After Judas left the communion table, they sang a hymn and left to their secret place to pray but Judas knew the place (Matth.26:30, 36-46). He should have been in prayer meeting with the team, but he was out doing mischief instead. For more on Judas, see volume 2, JUDAS ISCARIOT, *The Autopsy of a Betrayer.*

The Package Delivered

This is not a spy novel or movie, but the script is similar, even better. Remember, Judas was Satan's insider on the ministry team of Jesus. Judas voluntarily went to Caiaphas's murdering team and asked to be paid to deliver Jesus.

Judas had been paid, and now he delivers the goods. The prayer meeting in Gethsemane being ended, Jesus and His disciples exited the garden, and there he was! "Judas…with a great multitude with swords and clubs, came from the chief priests and elders of the people" (Matt.26:47).

Judas was absent from the Gethsemane prayer meeting because Satan entered him at the Last Supper table from which he excused himself to wrap up his betrayal deal with the enemies of Jesus (John 13:21-31). Fully fallen from grace—the traitor was now guiding the arresting guards and curiosity seekers to the ministry's secret place of prayer. There Judas found his ministry colleagues outside the garden. He identified Jesus with the kiss of betrayal, and the guards arrested Him.

There was a brief *kerfuffle* caused by Peter. In his attempt to defend Jesus, Peter inflected damage on Malchus, the servant of the high priest, using a sword to cut off his ear (John 18:1-11). Jesus commanded Peter to put away his sword, and healed Malchus by reattaching his severed ear (Luke 22:51).

Judas fulfilled his obligation; he delivered the package for which he was paid into the hands of the religious authorities (John 12:12-14). Up to this point, the civil government had no knowledge of these happenings. The Temple had their own guards with power to arrest, and they exercised it.

From human perspective, everything went downhill for Jesus from this point on. He would remain in custody until He was executed. Yet, in the economy of God everything went according to schedule.

The plot of Caiaphas and his group paid off handsomely, better than they could have imagined. Thanks to the traitor, Jesus is now delivered into the hands of "Caiaphas, the high priest, where the scribes and elders were assembled (Matt.26:57).

The hunter caught his prey, but in the end, it was hunter who was really caught. Like Judas, Satan had Caiaphas and his group. Jesus was no man's prey. It was prophesied that He would not fight those who would arrest and kill Him. Isaiah declared seven hundred years earlier, "He was led as a lamb to the slaughter, and as a sheep before its shearers is silent, so he opened not his mouth" (Isaiah 53:7). Jesus surrendered His life without a fight for our redemption (John 3:16; Romans 6:23).

CHAPTER 5

THE FUTURE OF THE TEMPLE PREDICTED

"Not one stone will be left upon another
that shall not be thrown down" (Matt. 24:1-3).

The people that wanted Jesus dead and plotted His death were religious people, most of them rich and powerful, and sat in high places of authority. They were not ignorant men but mostly respected scholars or teachers. They presided over the sacerdotal institution, namely the Temple, that they corrupted, and they were not willing to change because it was lucrative.

The Temple operation made the religious elite big money. But the Temple no longer served the purpose for which it was intended, and God was about to retire it. In fact, the Levitical priesthood, ceremonial laws, and animal sacrifice were never intended to be permanent but serve as a school-master leading people to the Christ or Messiah, the prefect One.

Christ arrived to find a corrupted system and tried to clean it up, but the custodians of the system strongly resisted Him. They set out to kill Him because He exposed their corruption and upset their Temple commerce. Yet, these men who opposed Jesus should have known He was the Messiah because they were the custodians of the revelation of God (i.e., the word of God).

This chapter, therefore, looks at God's vision for a new sacerdotal system that replaces the corrupted old system.

Jeremiah's New Covenant

From as far back as Moses, God promised to "raise up a prophet from among His people like unto Moses" (Deu.18:18). That prophet was the Messiah, the Seed of the Woman spoken of in Genesis 3:15; He was Abraham's substitutionary ram, and Isaiah's "Immanuel" ("God with us" (Isaiah 7:14). He would be Yahweh's suffering servant spoken of in Isaiah 53.

Jeremiah prophesied that the days are coming when God would establish a *new covenant* with the house of Israel and the house of Judah. This covenant would be different from the one He made with them when He delivered them from Egyptian bondage (Jer.31:31-46).

Jeremiah was referring to the covenant made with Israel under Moses at Sinai during the Exodus. The reason God gave for changing that covenant is that Israel did not keep it, "they broke my covenant" (verse 32). Deuteronomy 28 made it clear that the covenant was conditional. Faith and obedience were required. Israel would reap great blessings for obedience but suffer the curse of disobedience. Few of the main tenets of the *New Covenant* are given in the following paragraphs.

First, Moses and angels mediated the Old Covenant, but Jesus Christ would be the mediator of the New (Heb. 9:15). This alone makes the New Covenant superior to the Old. Moses and angels are servants of God, but Jesus is the Son of God (Hebrews 1:1-3:6). Who is greater in the house, a son or servant?

Second, the laws of the New Covenant are not written outwardly on tables of stones as the Old Covenant but written inwardly on the *hearts* and *minds* humans (Jer.31:33). Jesus became incarnate to establish the rule of God in humans' hearts.

Third, the Law of Moses was ratified by Jesus and compressed into one law; the law of love. Love for God and love for neighbor. Neighbor is redefined to include all fellow humans, not just the person living next door or just your own kin or race. For these changes see the Sermon on Mount (Matthew 5-7) and the *New Command* of Jesus (John 13:34-35; 1John 4:7-21). Most ceremonial laws have become o*bsolete* or optional (Heb.8:12).

Fourth, the New Covenant has a change of sacrifice. The Old Covenant had animal sacrifices offered for sins; it had to be repeated year after year because it could not remove sin or its guilt (Heb.10:1-10). Animal sacrifice was a temporary fix to shield worshipers from divine wrath, until the true sacrifice came in the person of Jesus Christ.

So, Jesus Christ is that true sacrifice. Before He was born, God instructed Joseph, "not to be afraid to take Mary as his wife for that which is conceived in her is of the Holy Spirit, And she will bring forth a Son, and you shall call His name Jesus, for he will save His people from their sins" (Matt.1: 20-21 NKJV).

At the Jordan River, John the Baptist introduced Jesus to Israel as "the Lamb of God who takes away the sin of the world!" (John 1:29-30). The apostle Paul reminds us that Jesus Christ is our "Passover Lamb that was sacrificed for us" (1 Cor. 5:7). The book of Hebrews refers to Christ as a "better sacrifice" and a *permanent sacrifice* because He is effectual and is offered only once and forever (Heb. 9:26-28, 10:12-14).

Fifth, the New Covenant has a changed of priesthood. We have shown in a previous chapter how corrupted the Levitical priesthood had become. God installed the priesthood through Moses and restricted it to the family Aaron. By the time of Christ, the high priest position was a political appointment.[1]

The imperfection of the Aaronic priesthood was evident from the golden calf fiasco (Exodus 32). It was Aaron the people coerced to build them a god that they could see; a god to take them back to Egypt. Later, two of Aaron's sons who were priests under his supervision died because they offered strange fire before God in worship (Lev.10: 1-10).

Much later still, God's judgment fell upon the house of Eli. He was high priest and his two sons, Hophni and Phineas, were priests under him. These two young men were corrupted, and they desecrated the priesthood, and Eli did not restrain them (1Sam.2:12-17). They all died horrifically the same day, including the wife of one of the sons (1 Sam.4:12-22).

The whole nation was endangered because of a corrupted, backslidden, and immoral priesthood back then. Israel's army was routed by their enemies, the Ark of God taken, and the glory of God's presence disappeared from the nation. They called it Ichabod; "the glory has departed" (1Sam.4:19-22).

This signals to us that a corrupted, backslidden, and immoral church can have serious national consequences for a people, economically, and militarily. It is one important lesson nations have not yet learned, and that includes the United States. Our economic and military strength are only sustainable when we have the favor of God (2 Chron. 7:12-14; Psalm 44:1-8).

Without the favor of God, the windows of heaven are closed, prosperity dries up, rain stops falling or falls too much, pestilence are released, crops fail, nature becomes disruptive, and other nations turn against us. This cycle was evident throughout Israel's history and is believed to be God's signature judgment for all times. It was from the Exodus to Malachi.

Malachi is the very last book of the Old Testament, and up to this time God had problems with a corrupted priesthood. It resulted in consequences for the whole nation. God rebuked the priesthood and charged them, even the whole nation for robbing His offerings, and sacrificing defective animals on His altar.

It was the duty of the priests to ensure that defective animals were not offered as sacrifices to God, but they neglected their responsibilities. And by reason of that their prosperity dried up and Malachi called the nation to repentance (Malachi 1-3).

When Jesus came on the scene He found a corrupted priesthood, overly commercialized to make a few rich. It was evident the old system, the old wineskin, could not contain the new win or teaching Jesus was offering to Israel. He tried to clean up the system, but they resisted Him hard (John 1:12). In the end, Jesus had to prophesy the dismantling of the old system and planned a new worship system in its place (Matt.16:13-20). This new system is the church, and Jesus is its heads and high priest (Eph.4:4-16; Heb.7:26-28).

Sixth, Jesus abolished the earthly high priest's position. In other words, He fired Caiaphas and took over his position. He took away the priesthood from the tribe of Levi and the family of Aaron. Jesus is the new high priest and chief priest combined. And His priesthood is of a different order, "the order of Melchizedek, a priesthood that predated the Aaronic priesthood (Compare Genesis 14:11-24 and Hebrews 6:20, 7:1-17).

Jesus has become "mediator" and "guarantor of a better covenant" (Hebrews 2:22). And a better priesthood.

Under the New Covenant, the entire body of believers constitute the new priesthood, and not one family but many. Ever believer in Jesus Christ is a priest, in the sense that each represents God to people, and people to God. The whole body of believers is the priesthood. The apostle Peter refers to the church as "a chosen people, a royal priesthood, a holy nation, God's special possession..." (1Peter 2:9).

So then, the body of believers is a fellowship of priests (Acts 2:47; 1John 1:3-7). For these reasons, a cardinal teaching of Baptist churches is: "We believe in the priesthood of all believers." This does not mean there is no need for pastors, deacons, or elders because Baptist recognize these offices.

The pastor or bishop is the under-shepherd whom the Holy Spirit has given the oversight of the church (Acts 20:28 ; 1Peter 5:1-4). That person is accountable to Christ for this work (Heb,13:7,17). And each believer is accountable to Jesus Christ and will appear at the Believers' Judgment (2 Cor.5:10).

Since our Lord Jesus Christ is the only high priest, He is referred to as being "behind the curtains" which is in heaven itself where we cannot see Him now. He is making intercession for His people (Heb.6:19-20). But one day, He will emerge from behind the curtains as the Old Covenant high priest used to do on the Day of Atonement. When Jesus emerges from behind the heavenly curtains, His people will behold Him face to face. That will be the glorious appearing of our "blessed hope" (Titus 2:11-15). That will also be the time for the consummation and glorification of our salvation (Rom.8:18-25, 31-39).

Just as the Old Covenant high priest was the only way to God, so Jesus Christ is the only way to God under the New Covenant (John14:4; Act 4:12). He is our mediator, advocate, propitiation, or mercy seat (Hebrews 4:16; 1John 2:1-2).

Seventh, the New Covenant has a changed of temple worship or sanctuary. This change was first forecast in Jeremiah's prophecy as a change to the human heart (Jer.31:33-34). Later, Jesus talked of this change in place and style of worship in His encounter with the Samaritan woman at the well (John 4:19-26). When she perceived that Jesus is a prophet, she pointed out that we Samaritans worshiped on the nearby Mount Gerizim (Deu.1:29, 27:12).

She continued, but you Jews worship at Jerusalem, Mount Zion. Jesus informed her that the time has come for true and sincere worship of the Father in the Holy Spirit (John 4:23-24). In other words, this quality of worship will not be restricted to a particular location, building, or race; it will be for all people, Jews and Gentiles.

CAIAPHAS The Pernicious High Priest

Under the Old Covenant, the Temple was central to the people of God; it was the primary place of worship. The place sacrifices were offered, the place God put His name, where He resided in the Most Holy Place. By law, the priests and the Levites controlled the Temple and all its activities. But that Temple had become seriously desecrated.

Nearly everything about the Temple was corrupted, hypocritical, done for show and the glory of men: prayer, fasting, giving to the poor (Matt.6:1-18). Those that controlled the Temple practiced a religion without compassion or mercy; their motivation was to amass earthly treasures for themselves (Luke 10:25-37; Matt.6:19-24). For these reasons, Jesus said to His disciples, "Except your righteousness exceeds that of the Scribes and Pharisees, you will in no case enter the kingdom of heaven" (Matt.5:20 KJV).

His disciples and other Israelites who worshiped at the Temple were proud of its architectural magnificence and imposing grandeur. But to Jesus this was a corrupted institution. Rather than being an instrument to facilitate authentic worship, it had become an object of worship itself, a monument of idolatry. Temple operators steadfastly resisted change because they regarded themselves as Abraham's seed. They thought that connection by itself guaranteed them eternal life, so they refused to repent (John 6:28-66). But God required faith and obedience.

During the week of His passion, Jesus prophesied the utter destruction of the Temple. He said that "not one sone will be left upon another that shall not be thrown down" (Matt.24:1-3).

This prophecy was fulfilled in 70 AD when there was an uprising in Jerusalem, and the Roman general Titus was sent to put down the rebellion and restore order. The Jews furiously fought back, but eventually the wall was breached, the Temple burnt and demolished. Over a million Jews died from the revolt and ninety-seven thousand taken prisoners taken as prisoners.[2]

Judaism as it was practiced during the time of Jesus was no more; it was forever dismantled. No Temple has been rebuilt since, animal sacrifices have ceased, the Ark of the Covenant has disappeared, the Hebrew language died. Modern Judaism is a reinvention without the Temple, without sacrifice, without the Ark, without the shekinah glory, without the true Messiah.[3]

Since the Temple was not destroyed until several decades after the ascension of the Christ, let's go back and see what happened in the interim. Jesus by His death and resurrection installed a new system called, the New Covenant. It gave birth to a new movement called the Church which was intended to enjoin both Jews and Gentiles in one body. The church started as a purely Jewish movement which Caiaphas and the other old guards of Judaism sought to eradicate without success. The old system, though dead spiritually, continued for several decades until it met its demise in AD 70.

What is the new temple under the New Covenant? If you recall, Jumeriah 31:33-34, God made it clear that under the New Covenant He would write His laws inwardly, upon the minds and hearts of people. The new temple, therefore, is the individual body of the redeemed, and collectively body of believers (1Cor. 6:19-20, 12:12-31).

The New Covenant introduces a new and different way to approach God. We come to God through Jesus Christ, the one and only way. Jesus said, "I am the way and the truth and the life. No one comes to the Father except through me" (John 14: 6 NIV). No one can bypass the Son of God and find entrance to the kingdom of God (John 3: 16-21). Any teaching or preaching to the contrary is false and dangerous. There are not many or few ways to God; there is one way! (Acts 4:12).

In Jesus Christ, we do not need to be afraid of God as Old Covenant people were at Sinai. They could not come near to God; Moses talked to God and relay God's message to them (Ex. 19:10-25). Under the New Covenant, we are invited to draw near to God without being stricken with fear. We are invited to come boldly into the presence of God and angels (Heb.4:16,12:18-24).

Furthermore, under the New Covenant, we address God as our Father because we are now sons and daughters of His family (Matt.6:9; Rom.8:14-17).Under the New Covenant, we can worship God more acceptably because we "worship in Spirit and in truth" (John 4:24; Acts 2:38-39).

Uniqueness of New Covenant Worship

For emphasis, this section repeats a few of the points already made but with a slightly different twist to them.

First, the people of God are not restricted to any particular nationality or race. They are all who come to God through Jesus Christ in a salvation experience, be they Jews or Gentiles (Eph.2:11-22, 3: 4-21).

Second, worship is not restricted to any particular location or building such as the Temple. Jesus informs us that wherever and whenever two are three people come together in His name, He is present in their midst (Matt.18:19-20).

Third, authentic worship is done under the anointing of the blessed Holy Spirit. Worship is not about buildings, rituals, vestments, and pageantry. These have their place in the corporate worship, but they are not an end in themselves.

Worship is honoring God the way He wants to be honored. He sets the standard for how we approach Him. Because He is holy, we seek to be holy. We try to meet Him in a clean place, and we seek to be properly and decently attired (Isaiah 6:1-6).

But authentic worship is a very intimate spiritual experience; it involves the whole person (Rom.12:1-2). Worship is our love expression to God—we are directed to love the Lord our God with all our heart, soul, mind, and strength (Mark 12:30-31).

Under the New Covenant, the human body is the new temple where God resides through the Holy Spirit (John 4:22; Acts 2:1-4). For these and other reasons, we should keep our bodies healthy, morally, and physically clean (Romans 12:1-2).

The apostle Peter to whom Jesus first mentioned the church, speaks of each believer as a living stone in the corporate body in which Jesus is the foundation stone (1Peter 2: 4-9). Peter was not a building in Jerusalem presided over by Caiaphas or a religious city in Rome headed by a Pope. Peter was speaking of the individual and universal body of believers in Jesus Christ, irrespective of race, gender, or nationality.

CAIAPHAS The Pernicious High Priest

CHAPTER 6

CAIAPHAS IN THE DEATH AND RESURRECTION COVERUP OF THE CHRIST

The death of our Lord Jesus Christ can be looked at from three or four perspectives: who wanted Him dead, who carried out the killing, and who allowed the killing? If law enforcement were investigating such murder or killing today, they would at least want answers to these three fundamental questions. As we will see, the death of the Christ is unique.

We will look at all three plus one more in this chapter. We will also consider how the murderers, strict observers of the Law of God, got around the prohibition, "You shall not murder" (Exodus 20:13).

Who Wanted Jesus Dead

This first question is easily answered from the records of all four gospels, and it is already addressed in the previous chapters of this work. But for emphasis, we are revisiting the issue in this chapter with as little redundancy as possible.

First, the evidence in all four gospels, overwhelmingly show that the people who wanted Jesus dead were: Caiaphas, the high priest, the chief priests (which were seven), the elders of the people, and most members of the Sanhedrin (Matt.26:1-5,14-16; John 11:45-47). At least two members of the Sanhedrin were secret followers of Jesus: Nicodemus and Joseph of Araminta. They did not agree to the position of the Council to have the Nazarene killed (Luke 23:50-54; John19:38-42).

I also want to point out that some of the categories overlap. For example, an elder could be a scribe, pharisee and a member of the Sanhedrin at the same time, and perhaps, even one of the seven chief priests. Elders were not a clearly defined group.*

These were the people who stood to gain materially from the demise of the Nazarene. They were the people mostly angered by His teachings, healings, and other activities. And these are the same people who were the gatekeepers of Jewish heritage and traditions; they managed the Temple institution.

Second, these were the same people who expressly plotted to kill Jesus, beginning with the raising of Lazarus (John 11:45-49). There were attempts to trap Him before this, but the Lazarus event caused them to formulate a fool proof plan to kill.

Third, these same religious leaders were the ones that financed the betrayal entrapment and called the money paid "blood money." Matthew gives us this intelligence report: "Then one of the twelve—the one called Judas Iscariot—went to the chief priests and asked, 'What are you willing to give me if I deliver him over to you?' So, they counted out to him thirty pieces of silver. From then on Judas watched for an opportunity to hand him over" (Matt.26:14-16).

Fourth, these were the same Jewish leaders that ordered the arrest of Jesus. There was a standing warrant issued shortly after Lazarus was brought back to life from the dead. Perhaps a new warrant was now issued. The victim would be brought to the ones who gave the arrest orders (Matt.26:47-57).

Fifth, they were the same folks who sought for witnesses to testify but they proved false. They conducted the religious trial which concluded with a charge of death for blasphemy. They later charged Him with treason against the Roman government because it gave them cover (Matt.26:59-68).

Sixth, they were the same ones that called for a civil trial before the Roman governor because they knew the common folks would not settle for stoning Jesus on a blasphemy charge.

*Seven*th, they were the same folks who persuaded the governor to crucify Jesus, despite His innocence (Matt. 27:1-2,12-26). The apostle John who was present at these proceeding captures the persistency of the religious leaders demanding the death of the Nazarene (John 19:1-16.).

At the cross the chief priests continued to pressure the governor what to write as the charge for which Jesus was crucified but at this point the governor being disgusted, refused to cave in to their pressure anymore (John 19:19-22).

Eight, this was the same group who paid off the soldiers to coverup the resurrection of Jesus and to tell a different story, using the talking-points given them as substitute for the truth (Matt.28:11-18).

Who Carried out the Killing?

The Roman governor repeatedly found Jesus to be innocent of the charge of treason and wanted to release Him. When they objected, he had the victim scourged, believing that they would have calmed their passion and satisfied their desire for death.

But again, they objected. The governor then offered to issue a pardon to release a prisoner, as was customary to do this time of the year (Passover). Pilate had Jesus in mind but again, they objected, proposing the release of the notorious criminal, Barabas, instead (Matt.27:24-26).

At one point, a basin of water was introduced, and the governor washed his hands from this demand for him to participate in the shedding of innocent blood. But they shouted, "Let His blood be upon us and upon our children" (verse 25).

This was amazing because these religious authorities knew that there was a curse attached to the shedding of innocent blood (Gen.4:10-12). At this point, the governor should have had the army clear the streets of this blood-thirsty mob and release the Nazarene that he already ruled, innocent. But he did not do that, he hesitated!

Finally, the mighty high priest toss a political hand grenade at the governor. He said, "We have no king but Caesar; if you let this man go, you are not Caesar's friend" (John 19:11-12). What the high priest was saying in substance, we can have Caesar recall you. In the face of this treachery, the governor capitulated and handed over Jesus to be crucified (verses 13-16). Political expediency prevailed over justice.

Under Roman law, Caiaphas and his cronies did not have the authority to render a civil execution of Jesus. But under Jewish law, he could have had Jesus stoned to death when he himself condemned Jesus to death at the religious trial before the Sanhedrin. But Caiaphas was too savvy a high priest and politician to go that route. He knew Jesus was too popular with the common people and they would have caused a riot.

With a riot on his hand, the governor would have stepped in with the army to squash such uprisings. Caiaphas wanted a civil trial as a cover, preventing such uprising of the common people. And even if there were an uprising, the governor would have exempted the religious elite. Because they would not be viewed as the cause of the riot because they were the ones that arrested Jesus and brought Him to Pilate for trial. These men were clever religious and political chess players. But they were not clever enough for heaven because they drove the nail in the coffin of their own religion, rendering it useless.

There are Jews today who refuse to read the New Testament record of their ancestors' involvement in the death of Jesus. There are those who want to hide behind the Romans. "The Romans killed Him, they say. But the records clearly show that the Roman did not want Jesus dead. The high priest, the chief priests, and elders, including the Sanhedrin wanted Him dead and plotted His death, and they were all Jewish. The Romans were the hands that carried out what Caiaphas and his group wanted.

Who Allowed the Killing?

The third perspective is the hand of God in the death of His Son. The very golden text of the Bible tells us that "God so loved the world that he gave his one and only Son, that whoever believes in him should not perish but have eternal life" (John 3:16). But before we discuss this perspective, we need to clear the deck of any prevailing misconceptions.

First, God's involvement in His Son's death does not exempt Caiaphas and his group of their wickedness or exempt Judas of his betrayal activities. They are all culpable, guilty of murder, and God will judge them at the place and time of His own choosing, unless they have repented and received His forgiveness. And don't think they can take cover under Jesus' prayer from the cross that says, "Father forgive them, for they know not what they are doing" (Luke 23:34).

This prayer appears to cover the soldiers who were merely following orders. The head soldier, a centurion, said of Jesus, "Surely, this man was the Son of God!" (Matt.27:54). The religious leaders of all persons were not ignorant men; they knew what they were doing!

Second, God did not cause anyone to do what they did to fulfill any prophesy concerning His Son's death. God giving His Son and the conspiring of wicked men to plot and carry out His murder are two separate things. The untrained mind in biblical matters may find it difficult to comprehend but that is the case.

Here is one simple illustration. God using Joseph to save many lives in Egypt, did not exempt his wicked brothers from wanting to murder him, and eventually sold him into slavery. His brothers meant it for evil, but God used it for His good purpose (Gen.50 15-21). We now turn to the hand of God proper.

The death of Jesus Christ was a sacrifice by God to God for the redemption of the human family (Isaiah 53:4-10; John 3:14-16). It was along this perspective that Jesus said, "No man takes my life from me, I have power to lay it down and power to take it up again." Or "destroy this temple and I will raise it up in three days." In both cases, Jesus refers to His ability to lay down His life and pick it up again. That was exactly what he did on Good Friday. He lay down His life and picked it up again on Easter.

This confirms that He is both human and divine at the same time. But all that does not give absolution to the wicked, murderous high priest, chief priests, elders, Sanhedrin, Pilate, and anyone else who plotted the death of Jesus of Nazareth in first century AD Jerusalem. Yet, anyone among them that truly repented and accepted Jesus Christ as Savior and Lord has received absolution and will not be thrown into hell but is welcome into God's eternal kingdom (John 3:16).

There is a fourth perspective on the death of Christ which does not cancel out any of the previous three. This perspective is that all of us, sons of Adam and daughters of Even killed Jesus of Nazareth. The apostle Paul writes, at the right time, "When we were still powerless, Christ died for the ungodly.... God demonstrates his own love for us in this While we were still sinners Christ died for us" (Romans 5:6-8).

The Resurrection Cover Up

Any law enforcement entity will tell you that those who are guilty of a crime or stand to gain most from a crime are the ones that are most likely to cover up or justify that crime. Caiaphas and his team not only wanted Jesus dead, but they also wanted Him to stay dead, not come back to life like His friend Lazarus. They were going to kill Him again if that happen, so let's seal the tomb and post guards there to ensure that this deceiver stays dead. Matthew gives us the following intelligence reports:

> The next day, the one after Preparation Day, the chief priests and the Pharisees went to Pilate. 'Sir,' they said. 'We remember that while he was still alive that this deceiver said, 'After three days I will rise again.' So, give the order for the tomb to be made secure until the third day. Otherwise, his disciples may come and steal the body and tell the people that he has been raised from the dead. This last deception will be worse than the first. (Matt.27: 62-64)

This is part of Caiaphas' group. They requested the governor to issue an executive order, to seal the tomb and post guards to enforce that order by watching the tomb. Pilate granted the request (verses 65-66,). We are familiar with this behavior in our time. When governments are afraid of being implicated in some crime, they are quick to seal files to prevent the public from knowing the truth. But they always do it in the name of protecting the innocent. The fact is, they are afraid of the truth.

But truth cannot stay buried; like oil, it will always rise to the surface.

Jesus said, I am the truth and the life. Every attempt by those first century religious murderers to contain Jesus failed, because the hand of the Almighty will aways prevail over wicked and conniving behaviors of religious and governmental elites.

The resurrection of Jesus was an earthshaking event, powerful with lights, blinding and glorious. Matthew tells us that a "violent earthquake" took place, that an angel of the Lord descended from heaven and rolled back the stone and sat upon it. His appearance was like lightning and his clothes were white as snow. The guards were so afraid of him that they shook and became like dead men" (Matt.28:1-8).

Dead men don't stand upright, so if the guards became like men, they were not only stiff with fear, but they were also clearly knocked off their feel in the presence of divine glory, consistent with similar happenings (Matt.17:1-8; Rev.1:17-18).

When the guards at the tomb regained their composure, they ran like scared cats to report what had happened to the chief priests and elders of the people (Caiaphas's' group).These men "devised a plan" to cover up the truth. They paid a large sum of money to the guards not to speak of what happened, but to repeat only the talking points they were given (Matt.28:11-15).

This alone has the markings of fraud, a cover up, written all over it. People are not normally bribed to tell the truth. The truth carries no baggage, no dressing up; it is the naked truth. Perhaps that's why the truth sets you free.

The religious elite and the government released a false story to the public. Millions that share Caiaphas' lineage continue to believe the lie he manufactured rather than read the full story from the New Testament. Many have followed Caiaphas' lie to the gates of hell itself. They have died without hope.

There are millions of Caiaphas' ancestors who have bought and advanced the lie throughout the centuries to date, yet the naked truth can easily be gleaned from the Word of God.

Eventually, the Gentile arm of the Church grew, and the Jewish arm diminished. Gentiles then persecuted Jews for the death of the Christ and the two continued their journey apart from each other to date. But that was never the intent of the Christ.

CHAPTER 7

JUDAISM WITHOUT TEMPLE AND SACRIFICE

Judaism as it was practiced during the time of Christ in first century Israel, officially ended with the destruction of the Temple by the Romans in AD 70.[1] That system is dead.

Judaism was an interdependent system of laws, priesthood, sacrifice, elders, and Temple. Since everything in the system revolved around the Temple, once it was destroyed and the priesthood taken, the rest crashed like a house of cards.

Jerusalem, the location of the Temple, was a citadel with walls; once thought to be impregnable. But it was breached, then knocked down, the Temple burnt and demolished, and the city ransacked. Many Romans died taking the city, and thousands of

Jews killed defending it, and thousands more were taken prisons of war.[2] Judaism was not just decapitated; it was demolished and will never recover to that level ever again. It served its purpose.

Furthermore, the Ark of the Covenant, the symbol of God's presence with His people disappeared; it has not been seen since. It was perhaps destroyed. Its disappearance signals that the glory has departed from Israel (Ichabod) as it was during the high priesthood of Eli (1Samuel 4:18-22). This time permanently; it is the judgment of God upon a backslidden nation. But it does not mean that God's plan for His ancient people was terminated; no, God still has big plans for Israel (Romans 9-11).

There Were Warning Signs

The destruction of the Temple and Judaism was the judgment of God against a corrupted system. But God never bring judgment upon His people without first giving them persistent warnings.

Judaism did not fall apart overnight; there were structural cracks from the rumblings of previous warnings that were ignored. Despite the warnings, Israel refused repentance. A brief look at its history reveals these warnings.

First, the nation had a history of covenant-breaking. They were a covenant people; they said, "Yes," to the covenant with Yahweh at Sinai under the leadership of Moses (Exodus 19: 7-9). The covenant was renewed with the second generation of the Exodus in Deuteronomy (*second law*). The blessings and curses of the covenant are summarized in Deuteronomy 28.

Second, Israel's national sin was persistent idolatry. Shortly after the death of Joshua through the time of the Judges, Israel engaged in idolatry (Judges 2:11-23). When a covenant people persistently fail to abide by the terms of the covenant, the blessings dry up and the curse of the covenant is released. That was what happened to backslidden Israel in the time of the Judges and throughout their history as a people. The constant refrain during the period of the Judges was, "And the children of Israel did evil again in the sight of the Lord again" (Judges 3:7, 12, Judges 6:1,10: 6, 13:1).

This frequent backsliding resulted in God delivering them into the hands of foreign powers that severely punished them until they repented and cried out to God for help. At that point, God would raise up a deliverer to champion their cause. This was their persistent pattern: backsliding through idolatry, the judgment of God, repentance, and deliverance.

Samuel, the last of the Judges, was called by God to lead Israel because the priesthood under Eli and his sons had become corrupted and immoral (1Sam.2:12-17). Eli, the high priest, failed to restrain his wicked sons who were priest under him. It was during this time that God spoke to the boy Samuel that He was going to bring judgment upon the house of Eli and upon the nation (1Sam.3-4).

The timeless lesson is this—a corrupted church, clergy or priesthood then and now brings God's judgment upon a nation. King Solomon warns, "Righteousness exalts a nation, but sin is a disgrace to any people (Prov.14:34).

Third, as the prophet Samuel was coming to the end of his tenure as judge, Israel requested a human king, so the nation transitioned from a theocracy (government under God) to become a monarchy (government under a king). Saul was the first king over Israel. Samuel anointed him to be king (1Sam. 9:37-10:1). Saul failed to follow God's directives as given by his spiritual advisor, Samuel. God rejected Saul for his disobedience and rebellion against Him. As a result, Saul's life was cut short; he and his son, Jonathan, died the same day (1Sam.31:1-6).

Years before Saul's death, Samuel secretly anointed the boy David to become king after Saul (1Sam.16:1-13). After Samuel's death, Saul learned of David's anointing and did everything in his power to kill David, but God did not allow it. David became king after Saul's death.

Despite David's many flaws, he was a man after God's own heart. He was the man God could work with. Israel has known no greater king than David. His son Solomon carried on with the Davidic dynasty. Solomon was a wise king, but he turned out to be a playboy in the end. His foreign wives brought idolatry into Israel and won over Solomon's heart (1Kings 11:1-13).

Because of his idolatry, God decided to rip the kingdom from Solomon's hand. But for David's sake, God would not do it in Solomon's lifetime (verse 13). This is generational blessing, but it has its limits, as you will see.

In fulfillment of the Word God, the nation was divided. After Solomon's death, his son Rehoboam came to the throne. Under his watch ten tribes fell away to form the Northern Kingdom, retaining the name Israel. Solomon's son, Rehoboam, was left with two tribes, Judah and Benjamin, which formed the Southern Kingdom, taking the name Judah (1Kings 12:1-24).

The Northern Kingdom was super-wicked; the lives of kings were cut short, so they were changed frequently. The worst were king Ahab and queen Jesebel. Jezebel destroyed the prophets and priests of Yahweh (God) and established her own religion of Baalism with its own priesthood and places of worship.

Through Elijah, God withheld the blessing of rain for three and a half years. The curse of famine burn through the land. Because of Jezebel, Elijah was in hiding but later emerged to face wicked king Ahab in a show-down of Gods of Mount Carme. The false god Baal and his priest loss the contest and were destroyed (1 Kings 18). Jezebel responded with a threat against Elijah's life (1Kings 19:1-10).

Due to persistent idolatry, the ten tribes of the Northern Kingdom came under the judgment of God. They were conquered by Assyria and carried off to that nation in 744 and 722 B.C. (2 Kings 15:29,17:5-6). They lost their identity and vanished from the earth into history. They are known today as the Ten Lost tribes of Israel. Of course, they are not lost to God.

In the process of time, the Southern Kingdom of two tribes became idolatrous as well. They were carried off to Babylon in several phases under Nebuchadnezzar; the last and most horrible was 586 BC. The Temple built by king Solomon was burnt and many people were taken to exile (Jer.52:1-30). They stayed in Babylon for seventy years. Only a remnant returned under Ezra to rebuild the Temple and under Nehemiah to rebuild the walls of Jerusalem. But even this remnant that returned, after a while, they, or the generation after them returned to idolatry.

The last prophet of the Old Testament is Malachi and the book that bears his name is addressed to a backslidden nation, included a corrupted priesthood (Malachi 1-2). The book includes a prophetic call to repentance, to honor God with their tithes and offering and God would again open the windows of heaven and flood them with blessings (Malachi 3).

Fourth Warning, John the Baptist. Jonn the Baptist was sent by God to prepare the people of Israel to receive the Messiah. You ask, why did they need to be prepared when they already had the written revelation of God, plus priests, prophets, and king? Israel was a backslidden nation with a corrupted priesthood. They had a false confidence that their blood connection with Abraham and Moses, though void of *faith and obedience*, guaranteed them a place in the kingdom of God. But family lineage does not qualify anyone for eternal life.

Abraham was a man of *faith and obedience*, they were not. They were persistent covenant-breakers. And God was ready to fulfill the Old Covenant through the coming of the Messiah and establish a *New Covenant* with the house of Israel and the house of Judah; one much different from the Old (Jer.31:31-36).

The New Covenant would be internal; it is the rule of God by the Holy Spirit in the hearts of His people. It would not be predicated on works and external rituals but on grace, faith, and obedience. It would be based upon better promises, a superior priesthood, and different Temple, not man-made but God-made. New Covenant spirituality is not based on biological connection with Abraham, but on a new birth experience in Jesus Christ.

For these reasons among others, John the Baptist came preaching, "Repent for the kingdom of heaven is at hand" (Mark 1:4-8). His mission was to prepare the way of the Lord. John made it clear that God was holding an axe at the root of the old tree (Judaism). He was going to cut it down and cast it into the fire because it was not fruitful tree (Matt.3:7-10).

Judaism lacked spiritual productivity. It turned out to be a barren frig tree, a false vine (Isaiah 5:1-7; Mark 11:12-13, 12:1-12). Israel was likened to a barren fig tree; it needed to be chopped down. Jesus said, "I am the true vine, and my Father is the vine dresser" (John 15:1). Any religion that denies that Jesus is the Messiah is a false vine.

The essence of John the Baptist's preaching was this—If the elite leadership of Israel did not take heed to the message of repentance to receive the Messiah, God would cut down the fig tree and inaugurate something new to in its place. John was not of the elite class; he was not sophisticated enough, so they ignored him and his message. Yet, many of the common people received John as a prophet of God.

Despite being ignored by the elite class, John the Baptist did introduce Jesus as the Messiah to Israel. (John 1:29-34). They did not receive him, nor heed his warnings as a prophet of God (Matt.21:23-27). They later rejected Jesus as the Messiah (John 1:12, 6:41-71).

Fifth Warning, Jesus and the Apostles. The mission of Jesus Christ was to give humans a fuller revelation of God and redeem them by the sacrifice of Himself (Matt.1:21; Heb. 2:9-11*).* God had put in place a structure He planned to transform, comprised of a godly nation, a priesthood, and a Temple. This structure was to receive the Missiah through whom the whole human family could receive God's plan of redemption (John 3:-13-18). God was building something much bigger than one little nation; He was building a family of nations.

But the entire structure of the model nation, priesthood, and Temple became corrupted. They refused all efforts to clean up the system. Finally, they rejected the Messiah Himself. The leaders of Judaism fought Jesus to keep the old wineskin which was inadequate to contain the wine of the New Covenant.

Yet, despite Israel's rejection, the Messiah still put in place an alternative and better method, now called the Church. It has a global rescue mission of redemption (Matt.16:13-19; 28:18-20). The old wineskin of Judaism was destroyed, even though the keepers resisted hard to keep it.

All four gospels revealed how Jesus emerged on the scene, preaching the same message as John the Baptist, "Repent for the kingdom of heaven is at hand" (Matt.3:1-12, 4:17). But His ministry approach was much different from John the Baptist's.

Jesus' message was more refined and scholarly. He took His message to the people. He accompanied preaching and teaching with healing, exorcism, vigorous debate, and a feeding program. Jesus spoke with greater authority and even put the elite scholars to shame. Jesus had a broader ministry than John the Baptist because His had more disciples and put them to work (Matt.4:23-25; 10:1-15). At one point, Jesus appointed seventy-two additional disciples and sent out to minister (Luke 10:1-17).

Jesus' offered salvation first to the Jews; His ministry was to the lost sheep of the house of Israel (Matt.10:5-6). His disciples were all Jewish. He was popular with the common people. But the elite class, the leadership of the people, the scribes, the pharisees, and the priesthood rejected Him, despite clear and convincing evidence that He was the Messiah.

Throughout His ministry, Jesus confronted the scribes and pharisees, the leadership class, for their unbelief and hypocrisy. He repeatedly warned and called them to repentance (Luke

11:47-54, 13:1-5). But instead of repenting, they plotted to kill Him, as shown in previous chapters of this book.

Jesus finally decided to destroy the old system. But this decision was reached during the week of His passion, after all efforts were made to change the system. They rejected Him and were now determined to kill Him. Jesus knew that once the Temple is destroyed, the system would come crashing down like a deck of cards. He sat on the Mount of Olives before His death and prophesied the destruction of the temple, the very citadel of Judaism (Matt.24:1-3).

But why didn't He destroy the Temple then and there, during the week of His passion? Because His resurrection and the witness the apostles would give Israel another opportunity to embrace Jesus as the Messiah and embrace the inauguration of the New Covenant. Animal sacrifice would have ended without the destruction of the Temple. Jesus Himself is the sacrifice that ends all sacrifices. The rending of the vail of the Temple while Jesus was on the cross signals this fact (Matthew 27:50-51).

The Apostles' Warning. The resurrection of the Christ gave the Jewish leaders another opportunity to reconsider what they had done, having Jesus crucified. But instead of repenting and coming clean, they doubled down on an elaborate scheme to make Him an impostor and cover up the truth of the resurrection.

The guards at the tomb that witnessed the resurrection were paid off and given talking points contrary to what happened. Who did this? The same elite leadership of Judaism that had plotted the death of the Christ, initiated, and carried out the resurrection cover up scheme (Matt.28:11-15).

CAIAPHAS The Pernicious High Priest

The witness of the apostles was the final opportunity for the leadership of Judaism to come clean. Jesus appointed the apostles to be witnesses of His life, death, and resurrection. The hope of both Jews and Gentiles rest on the bodily resurrection of Jesus Christ (1Cor.15:12-58). "For as in Adam all die, even so in Christ shall all be made alive" (verse 23).

Jesus commissioned His apostles to begin their witnessing in Jerusalem, then Judea, then Samaria, then to the ends of the world (Acts 1:8). Who lived in Jerusalem and Judea? Jews! Samaria? Half Jews (a mixed race). So again, Jews were given the first opportunity to hear the gospel and receive eternal life.

Did the apostles carry out the order? Yes, they did! Peter on the Day of Pentecost preached to Jews from all over the Roman Empire who had come to Jerusalem for that Festival (Acts 2:1-36). Using quotes from the Hebrew Scriptures, Peter pointed out to them that Jesus whom the elders of the people ignorantly crucified was indeed the Messiah sent by God to redeem Israel. Here is Peter's clinching point: "Therefore, let all Israel be assured of this: God has made this Jesus, whom you crucified both Lord and Messiah" (Acts 2:36).

What was the response to this cutting indictment? The leadership held their ground. But again, the common people were "cut to the heart and said to Peter and the other apostles, 'Brothers, what shall we do.' Peter responded, 'Repent and be baptized, every one of you in the name of Jesus Christ for the forgiveness of your sins. And you will receive the gift of the Holy Spirit' "(Acts 2:37-38). This response included several poor priests.

What was the immediate outcome? Three thousand souls accepted the message, got baptized, and were added to the Jesus' Movement that day (Acts 2:41). So, the Church got started as a Jewish movement in a Jewish city, Jerusalem, by the apostles of Jesus who were Jews themselves, but not of the elite class.

The Jesus movement did not include the leaders of the Judaism who had plotted the death of Jesus. They continued a counter narrative opposing, discrediting, and persecuting the movement. How do we know this? They emerged with renewed vigor to persecute the followers of Jesus and sought to stamp out the life of infant movement called, *The Way*.

With the healing of a crippled man at the gate of Temple in Acts chapter 3, Peter and John were arrested, beaten, and charged not to minister again in the name of Jesus. Who did this? The same group of leaders that plotted the death of Jesus and covered up His resurrection (Acts 4:1-21). Then they stoned Stephen to death; he was one of the seven deacons appointed in the six chapter of Acts (Acts 7:54-60).

This started a full-scale persecution against the followers of Christ in Jerusalem, so many fled to other cities (Acts 8:1-3). About this time, Saul of Tarsus received warrants from Caiaphas, the high priest, to arrest followers of Christ from city to city and bring them in chains to Jerusalem for trial and imprisonment. On one of these missions, the risen, ascended, and glorified Christ apprehended Saul on the Damascus Road (Acts 9:1-19). From this day onward, Saul the hunter became one of the hunted (Acts 9:20-31).

Later, king Herod wanted to score political points with the Jewish leaders, had James, a prominent apostle and brother of

John killed with the sword. Herod observed that his murderous action was pleasing to the Jewish leaders, so he had Peter arrested, placed in chains, and thrown into prison. He wanted to do Peter as he did to James (Acts 12:1-4). But this time the Church fought back; a prayer meeting was called to pray for Peter's deliverance from prison (verse 5).

The power of prayer moved heaven, and an angel was sent to release Peter out of Prison. The prison was still closed, guards on duty, but when they opened the prison Peter was gone (Acts 12:6-18). It's like he was Houdinied away, but this was no magic; it was God protecting His servant from wicked men.

The prison guards were interrogated and put to death by Herod, but he left Peter alone; heaven had Peter covered. Later an angel struck king Herod and worms ate him alive until he died (Acts 12:19-23). Those who opposed God are fighting a losing game and will come to a bitter end. But the Word of God will increase and bring a great harvest of souls (verse 24).

So, the persecutor and hit man Saul (his Hebrew name), whom Caiaphas hired to hunt down followers of Jesus Christ, was converted to Jesus Christ and became the Jesus Movement's most ardent and charismatic leader (Acts 13:1-4). It is most interest that Paul (his Greek name) in his missionary journeys from city to city, always gave the first opportunity to the Jews to hear the gospel and receive Jesus as Messiah (Romans 1:16-17).

Paul always began his preaching at the synagogue (Acts 13:4-5, 14-16, 42-49). But the counter narrative that Caiaphas and his cronies had spawned spread like wildfire and more Jews kept rejecting the Messiah and the message of salvation. After a while the church became a predominantly gentile movement

(Acts 13:50-52). Despite many attempts on his, Paul kept going to the synagogue first when he entered a new city, thus giving Jews the first opportunity at salvation (Acts 14:1-19).

He continued that pattern to the day of his death because he was convinced the gospel was to the Jew first (Roman 1:16-17). Paul gave the gospel of salvation to both Jews and Gentiles; both are without excuse before God (Romans 2:1-11).

The sixth and final warning nails the Coffin of Judaism. Since, the crucifixion and resurrection of Jesus Christ, God has made it clear that Judaism without the Christ is no longer an authentic religion; it does not provide the way to salvation from sin or gives eternal life. A Jew reading this by itself today, will become horrified, and will even label it antisemitism. But this is the honest, indisputable truth that must be spoken boldly in love.

This does not mean Judaism does not have value; it has great value for this life. But without Christ, it has no value for the life to come. But if the Jew goes one step beyond rituals to embrace Yeshua as Savior, Lord, Messiah—his religion becomes more than a rich cultural heritage to celebrate. He has salvation from sins, even eternal life. Eternal life is through Christ alone! You cannot dismiss Jesus and have eternal life (John 3:16; Acts 4:12).

Despite their rejection of Jesus Christ, God has not cast away the Jewish people; at least, a remnant will be saved, at most all Israel. God is not finished with the Jew or Israel. The apostle Paul addressed the Jewish question in Romans chapters 9 to11. Paul made it clear that *God has not cast away His people whom He foreknew* (Romans11:1-2), that the spiritual blindness of Israel is temporary, until the fulness of the Gentiles is brought into the kingdom, then all Israel will be saved (Rom.11:25-26).

The authentic Jewish people who are alive upon the earth when Yeshua returns, will have the opportunity to embrace Him as their Messiah, Savior, and Lord. The evidence will be so overwhelmingly convincing that all Israel will embrace Him and be saved. Jews who embrace Yeshua now, during the church age, are already saved (John 3:16). We call them Messianic Jews.

When Messiah returns, He will be the same person their ancestors rejected, crucified, and scorned throughout the centuries. During the time of Jacob's trouble or the Great Tribulation, God will seal one hundred and forty-four thousand (144,000) Jewish messengers to preach Christ to unbelieving Jews, to prepare them as a people to receive Yeshua as their Savior, Lord, Messiah at His Second Advent (Revelation 7:1-8, 14:1-5). (See Vol.1 and 3 the series by this author, *"Related Events to the Second Coming of the Christ*).

Let me emphasize, Jews who embrace Yeshua now as Savior, Lord, Messiah have eternal life (John 3:16-18). They are part of the Church as the apostles were. Jesus made it clear that both believing Jews and believing Gentiles would become one body in Christ, one flock under one shepherd (John 10:14-16).

The apostle Paul also emphasize this unity of one body in Christ (Eph.2:14-22). God gave the full revelation of this mystery to Paul, a Jew who became apostle to the Gentiles (Eph.3:1-21). Any Jew or Gentile who dies now or at any time in the church age without knowing Jesus as Savior, Lord, Messiah is lost. There is no salvation outside of Christ (John 3:16-18; Acts 4:12).

Now, let's discuss the term "the final nail in the coffin Judaism" used at the beginning of this section. The destruction of the Jewish Temple in Jerusalem by the Roman in AD 70, fulfills the prophesy of Jesus that "not one stone will be left upon another that shall not be thrown down" (Matt.24:1-3).

The prophecy was fulfilled in AD 70 when the Romans destroyed the Temple. From that date, Judaism ceased to be practiced the way it was practiced in the time of Jesus. For Judaism to be viable or authentic, it must have the following:

1. *The Temple*: the temple must be at the same location in Jerusalem. Jews have many places of worship today, including synagogues, but no authentic Temple.
2. *Authentic Sacrifice*: Sacrifice could only be offered in the Temple in Jerusalem but there is none. Some Jews in New York at times offer chickens, but they would be better off eating them. That is an exercise in futility.
3. *An Authentic Priesthood:* the Aaronic Priesthood is needed to offer sacrifice. But there is no priesthood.
4. *The Ark of the Covenant*: This unique piece of furniture symbolizing the presence of Yahweh (God) has disappeared with the destruction of the Temple.
5. *The Shekinah light of glory;* This was a shaft or beam of light from heaven the shone through the roof of the Temple in the Most Holy place over the Ark of the Covenant. Its appearance signals God acceptance of the sacrifice offered with its blood on the Mercy Seat.[3]

These five things are necessary for the authentic practice of Judaism, but they are lost; they are no more since the destruction of the Temple in AD 70. Is it not obvious that God has replaced the old system for something new? Yes, God has completely closed every path to bring back Judaism as it was once practiced in the time of Christ. Even the Hebrew language was lost. Notwithstanding, in AD 90 a few surviving Pharisees and rabbi got together to preserve the Jewish identity and that was the beginning of modern Judaism.[4]

The Tower of Babel is a reminder of history that humans like to go against God and when they do, confusion is the certain outcome (Gen.11:1-9). So, it would not be surprising if the adherents and sympathizers of Judaism want to push back against God, rebuilt a Temple, and reinstate state sacrifice. But God will never again accept animal sacrifice for the atonement of sins (Matt.1:21; John 1:29).

People may be foolish enough to offer animal sacrifices for their sins, but God will not and cannot accept them. Jesus Christ, the Lamb of God is that one and permanent sacrifice for all humans, Gentiles, and Jews alike (Heb.9:11-15, 28).

We humans always like to invent our own way of salvation rather than accept God's way. Paul, the apostle, refers to this inclination as being "ignorant of God's righteousness," as going about "establishing their own righteousness." They have not submitted themselves to the righteousness of God. "Christ is the end of the law for righteousness to everyone who believes" (Romans 10:1-4).

Therefore, bypassing Jesus Christ to secure eternal life, or to get into God's heaven is an exercise in futility. The Torah, the Prophets, the Writings, and all its practices were a temporary fix, as a schoolmaster to lead us to Christ, the perfect One.

We like the broad road to heaven with lanes to suit our particular lifestyle, but the true road to salvation from sin and to eternal life is a narrow road. And that is through Jesus Christ alone (Matt.7:13-14; John 14: 4).

Summary

The damage that Caiaphas, the high priest, the chief priests, the Sanhedrin, and elders of the people did against the Jewish people is incalculable. But the man that stands in the center of the circle of blame is God's high priest. He was God's representative to the people and the people's representative to God, but he failed on both counts. Under God, Caiaphas had the final word. His was to shout the loudest, "Crucify Him!" He was imposing the death sentence that he levied upon the Son of God earlier before the Sanhedrin (Matt.26:62-68).

Caiaphas and his group wanted Jesus dead, they plotted His death, they financed the betrayal, they had Him arrested and abused in custody. They tried the Son of God, charged Him as a blasphemer and imposter, and declared that he was worthy of death. They pressured the Roman governor to crucify Jesus, even though He was found innocent. Caiaphas and his group wanted Him crucified anyway and "let His blood be upon us and upon our children," they said (Matt.27:22-25).

Caiaphas, the seven chief priests, the elders, and most members of the Sanhedrin maliciously covered up the truth of the resurrection. They paid-off the guards to tell a false story (Matt.28:11-15). Later, Caiaphas had the followers of Jesus persecuted and made their lives hell to spread a false narrative about Jesus (Acts 7:1-3, 54-60, 9:1-4).

Because of Caiaphas's wickedness against God and our Lord Jesus Christ and the blessed Holy Spirit, God removed the corrupted, idolatrous system of Judaism from before Him: temple, priesthood, Ark of the Covenant, and animal sacrifice forever. But Caiaphas's children, generation after generation continue to advance a form of Judaism without Christ, but God cannot accept a worship system minus His Son (John 4:21-24; Acts 4:12). But despite their chronic unbelief, all are not lost God has prepared a believing remnant for Himself.

The irony is, despite the scholarship, the universities of higher learning, the Nobel Prizes won, unbelieving Jews continue to climb up into God's heaven through a path He does not approve. Yeshua said to Nicodemus, "no one can enter the kingdom of God except he is born again" (John 3:5). Yeshua is the gate or door to the kingdom (John 3:16). Jews will eventually come to the knowledge of the truth and be saved (Romans 11:1-6, 25-26). But at what cost!

Judaism without a temple and a sacrifice is Judaism without a Savior. A religion without a Savior is an exercise in futility; it leads to everywhere except heaven.

REFERENCES

Introduction:
1. Dewar, Michael W. JUDAS ISCARIOT, *The Autopsy of a Betrayer.* Brooklyn, NY: Dwelling Place Publishers. Vol.2, 2025.

Chapter 1
1. Flavius Joseph, *The Works of Josephus.* Translated William Whiston. Peabody, MA: Hendrickson Publishers, 1987, 539.
2. Merrill F. Unger. *The New Unger's Bible Dictionary.* Editor R.K. Harrison. Chicago, IL: Moody Bible Institute, 1988. 191.
3. *Ibid, 191.*
4. *Ibid, 191.*
5. Constantinou, Scarvelis Eugenia PhD. *The Crucifixion of the King of Glory.* Chesterton, IN: Ancient Faith Publishing, 2021, 146.

6. *Ibid.*
7. Ibid.

Chapter 2
1. *The New Unger's Bible Dictionary.* Entry: "Hebrew High Priesthood," 1030-32.
2. *Ibid.*
3. *Ibid*, 1030.
4. Ibid.
5. *Ibid*,1319
6. *The Crucifixion of the King of Glory*, 61.
7. *Ibid.*
8. *Ibid.*
9. I*bid*, 60.
10. *Ibid*, 60-61.
11. *Ibid.*
12. *The New Unger's Bible Dictionary,* 770.
13. *The Crucifixion of the King of Glory* King of Glory, 59.
14. *Ibid.*
15. *Ibid.*
16. *Ibid,* 62.
17. *Ibid*, 63.
18. King of Glory (Temple takes 86 years to build).
19. King of Glory, P.59
20. King of Glory, n

Chapter 3
1. *The New Unger's Bible Dictionary,* 375-74
2. *The Crucifixion of the King of Glory*, 44.
3. *Ibid*, 45.

REFERENCES

Chapter 4

1. *The Crucifixion of the King of Glory,* 134-35.

2. *Ibid*, 35.

Chapter 5

1. *The Crucifixion of the King of Glory, 134*

2. Schneider, Kirt A. Rabbi. *The Lon of Judah.* Lake Mary, FL: Charisma House. 2018, 42-43.

3. *Ibid.*

Chapter 7

1. Schneider, Kirt A. Rabbi. *The Lon of Judah.* Lake Mary, FL: Charisma House, 2018, 41-43.

2. *Ibid.*

3. *Ibid.*

4. Ibid, 43-44.

The star of David will never go out; it will shine forever, though somewhat flickering now.

OTHER BOOKS BY THIS AURHOR

Series 1: *Related Events to the Second Coming of the Christ* – 10 Volumes.

Vol.1

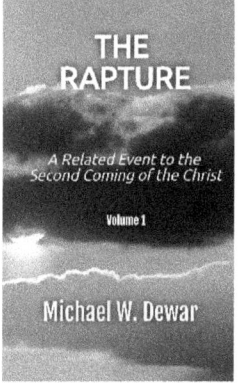

Vol.2

Vol.3

Vol.4

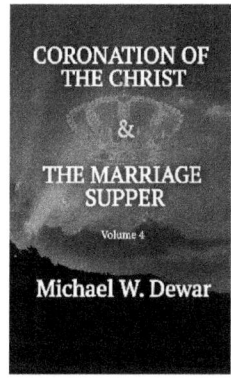

Vol.5

Vol.6

Vol.7

Vol.8

OTHER BOOKS BY THIS AUTHOR

Vol.9

Vol.10

Series 2: *Ready for the Coming Exodus*? 3 Volumes
(This series is not sequential; you can begin with any of the 3 books but preferably the one Heaven If you want In).

Vol. 1

Vol.2

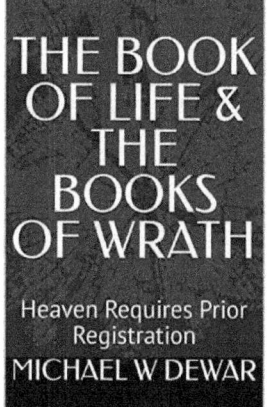

Vol.3

============

A Training Course in Conflict Management and Resolution for Churches. Launch a Peace Ministry in Your Church. Three volumes: Textbook, Instructor's Manual, and Students' Manual.

 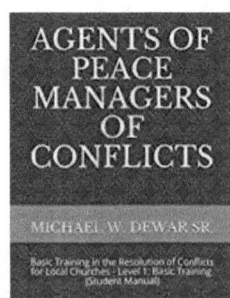 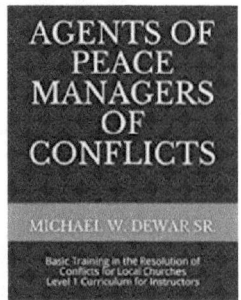

Textbook · Students' Manual · Instructor's Manual

ABOUT THE AUTHOR

Michael W. Dewar, Sr. is a pastor, Bible teacher, and mentor in the spiritual life. He is also a specialist in the resolution of church and family conflicts. He authors a course of study for training Agents of Peace, Ministers of Conflict for launching a peace ministry in each local church.

He holds earned degrees which includes a B.A., the Master of Divinity, the Master of Social Work with License from the State of New York, and a doctorate. Rev. Dewar pastors in New York where he lives with his family.

CAIAPHAS   The Pernicious High Priest

www.ingramcontent.com/pod-product-compliance
Lightning Source LLC
Chambersburg PA
CBHW071718040426
42446CB00011B/2112